SONATAS AND SONATINAS: CLASSICS TO MODERNS

Selected and edited by Denes Agay

Foreword

The sonata is not only the most important of all instrumental forms, but is also one of the great artistic achievements of human creativity. The form itself, which had been crystallized by Hayden and Mozart as the first section of a multi-movement work, is essentially a simple, A-B-A patterned musical structure (Exposition—Development—Recapitulation), which the mind grasps easily and which at the same time is sturdy and elastic enough to be the repository of an infinite variety of musical inventions and manipulations. The ten sonatas and six preparatory sonatinas contained in this volume present a varied cross section of this important literature from the Baroque to the present.

All works are in their original forms, based on authentic texts. Editorial additions either appear in small print or are referred to in footnotes. The grade level of the pieces is, by necessity, wide, from easy to difficult. As an approximate guide to grading the contents of the collection, the composers, each being represented by one work, my be listed in the following order: Schmitt, Reinecke, Gurlitt, C.P.E. Bach, Benda, Cimarosa, Sorokin, Agay, Scarlatti, Haydn, Clementi, Mozart, Beethoven, Schubert, Grieg, Kabalevsky.

We hope that this latest addition to the "Classics to Moderns" family of books will be as welcome and useful as have been its companion volumes of the series.

Denes Agay

Lithographed in U.S.A. by
EDWARDS BROTHERS INCORPORATED
2500 SOUTH STATE STREET / ANN ARBOR, MICHIGAN 48104

Consolidated Music Publishers
New York • London • Tokyo • Sydney • Cologne

Contents

For a graded sequence of the above works see foreword

International Standard Book Number: 0-8256-4067-9
Library of Congress Catalog Card Number: 73-92397

Distributed throughout the world by Music Sales Corporation:

33 West 60th Street, New York 10023
78 Newman Street, London W1
4-26-22 Jingumae, Shibuya-ku, Tokyo 150
27 Clarendon Street, Artarmon, Sydney NSW
Kolner Strasse 199, 5000 Cologne 90

SONATA

L. 23

Domenico Scarlatti

* All dynamic and staccato marks are editorial additions.

mf

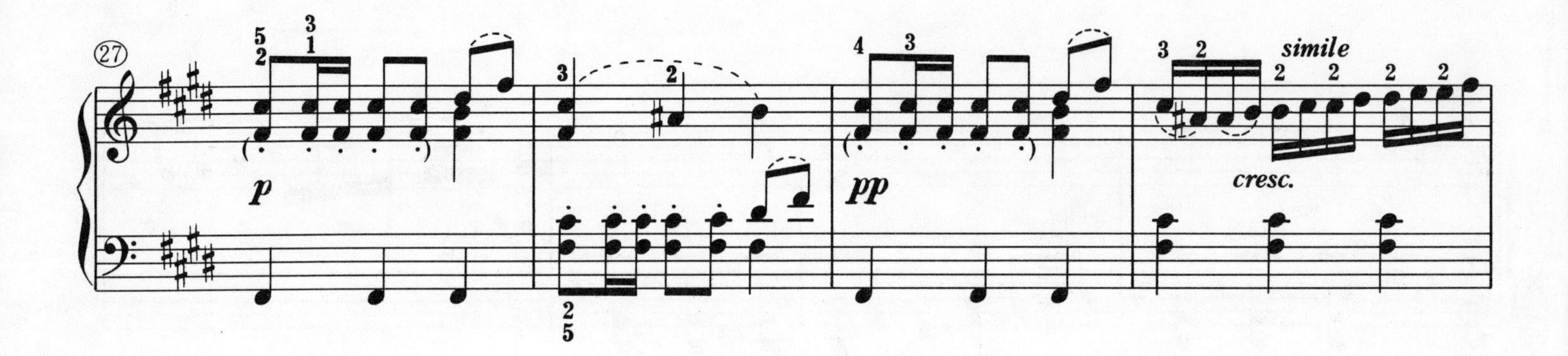
simile
p
pp
cresc.

mf
mf

p
mf
p

mf

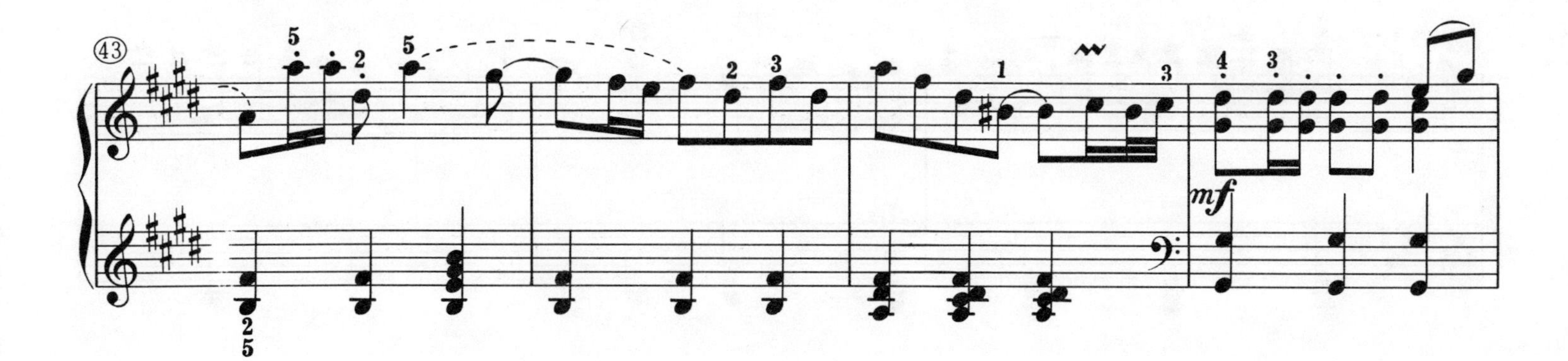
43
mf

47
p
cresc.

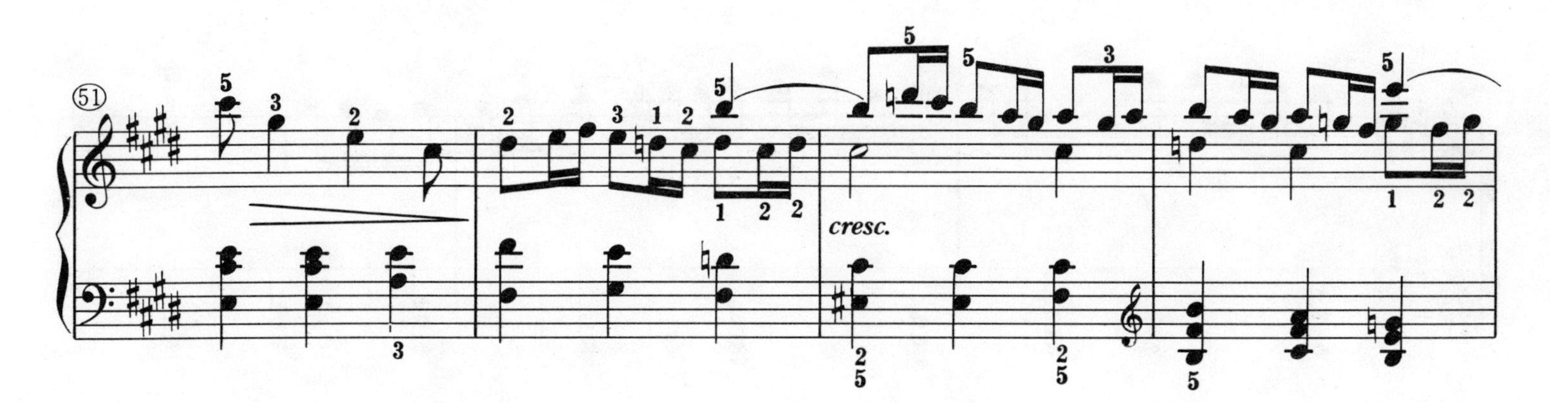
51
cresc.

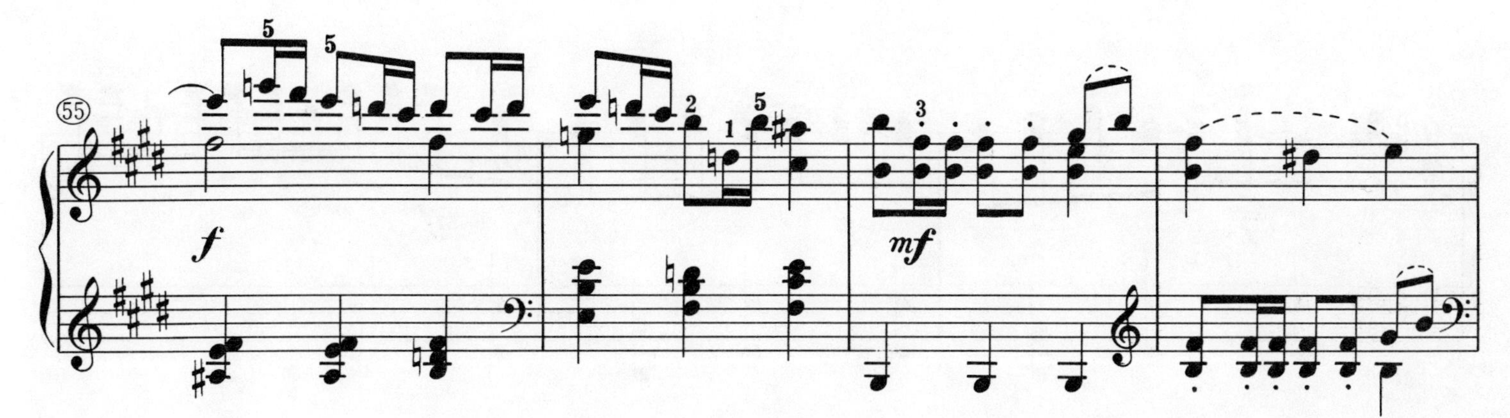
55
f
mf

59
p
simile
cresc.
mf

62

65
p
simile
pp
cresc.

69
mf

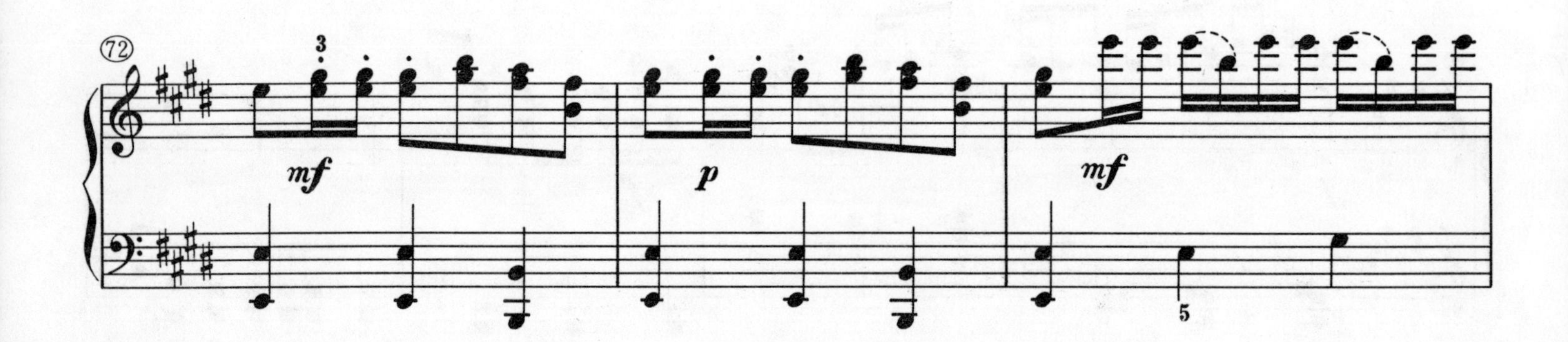
72
mf
p
mf

75
p

SONATINA
(No. 34)

Jiri Antonin Benda

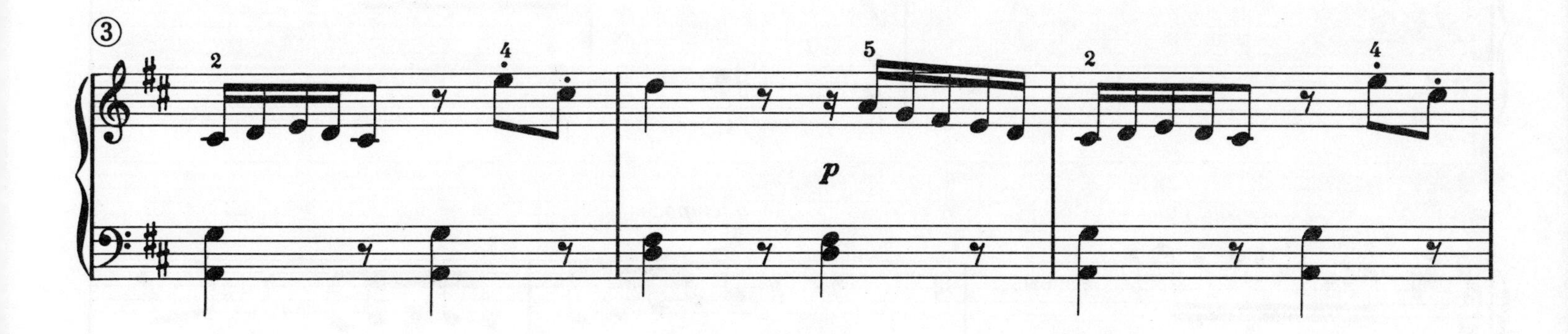

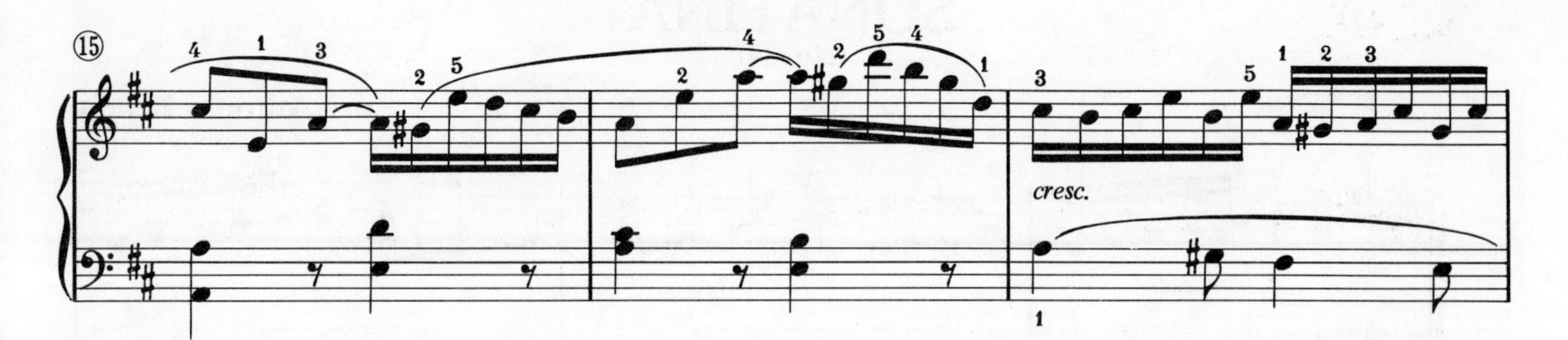
15
cresc.

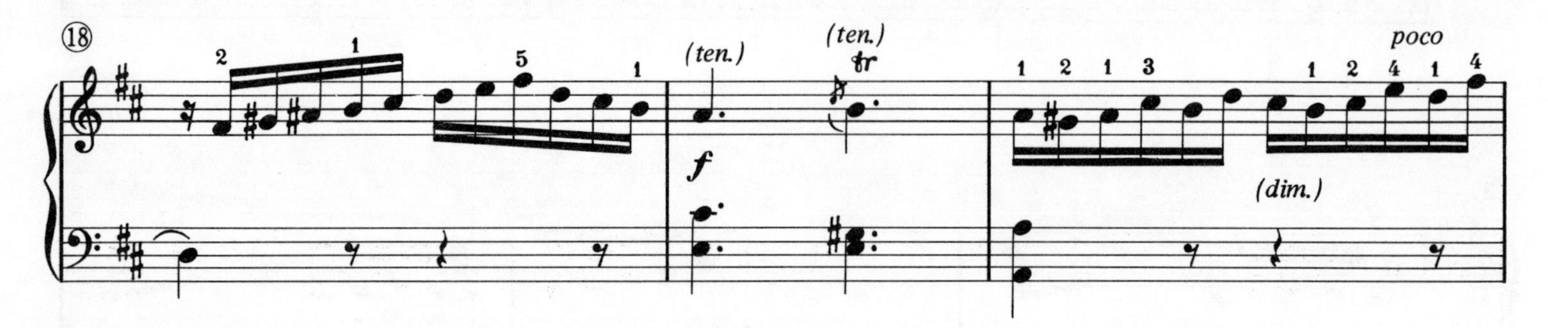
18
(ten.)
(ten.)
tr
poco
f
(dim.)

21
rit.
a tempo
f non legato

24
p

27

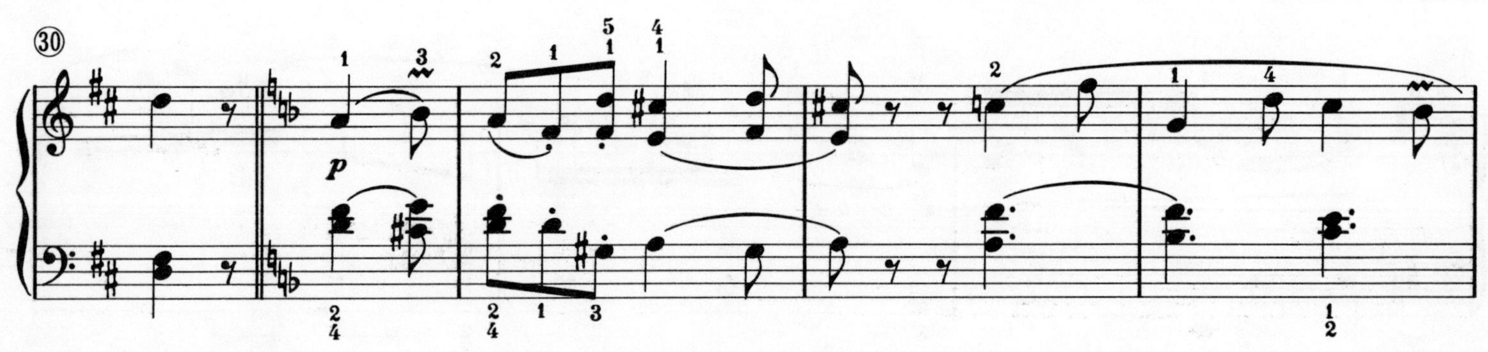
30
p

34

38
poco rit.
pp

41
a tempo
f non legato

44
p

47
f

SONATA

Allegro

Carl Philipp Emanuel Bach

26
(p)
(mf)

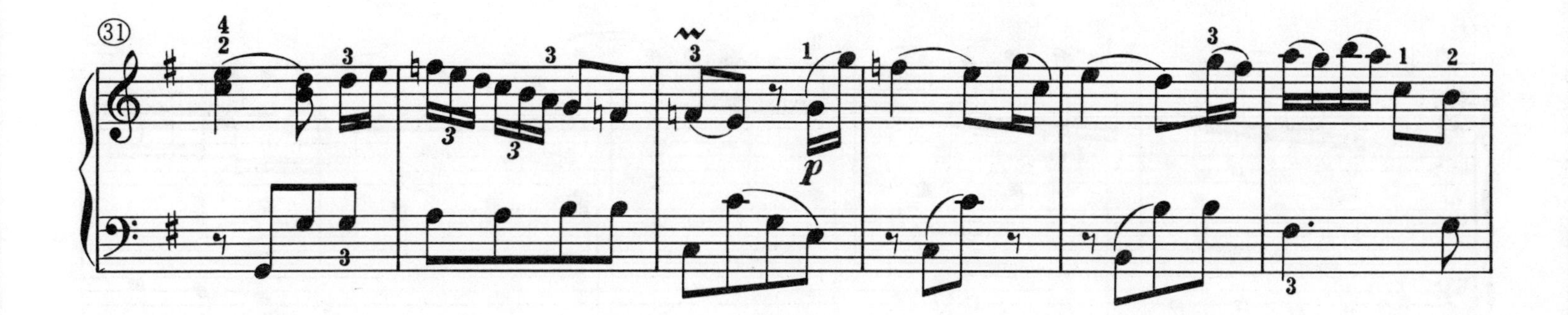
31
p

37
p
(cresc.)

43
(mf)
(cresc.)

48
f p
f

Andantino
(mp espress.)
p

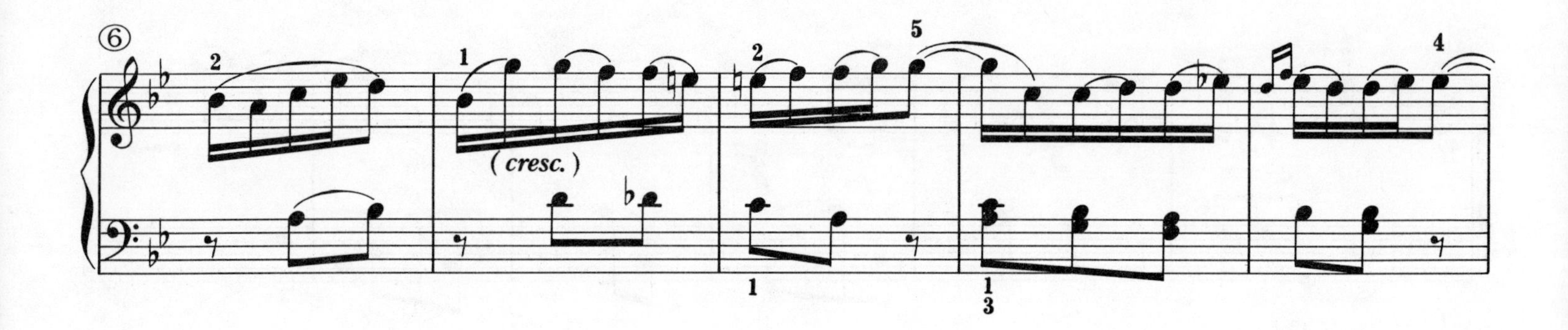
(cresc.)

(dim.)
mp

p
(cresc.)

(mf)
p

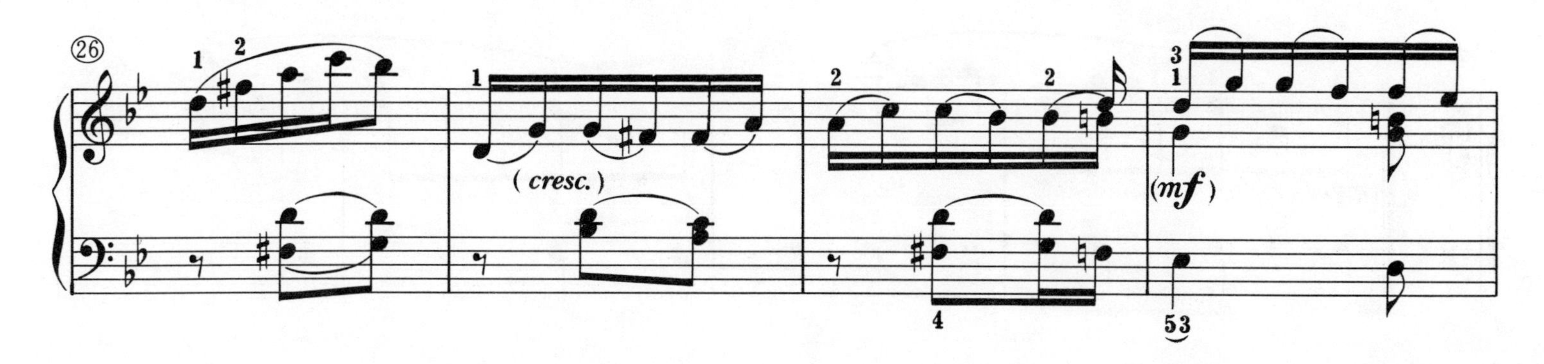

(cresc.)
(mf)

(dim.)

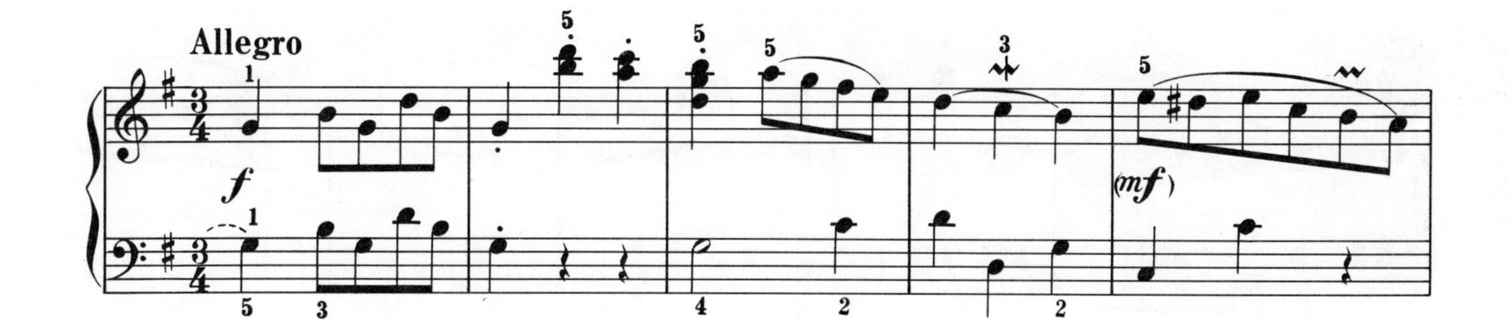

Allegro
f
(mf)

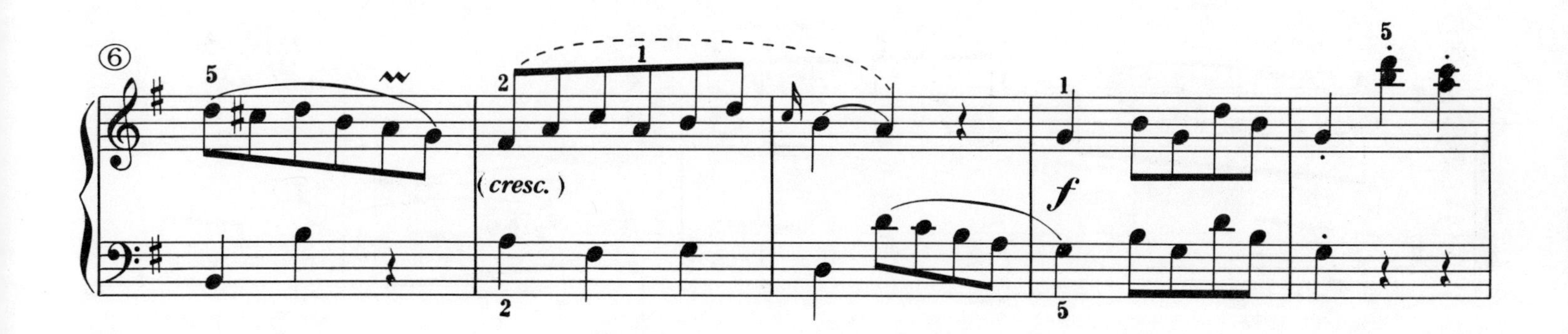

(cresc.)
f

(mf)

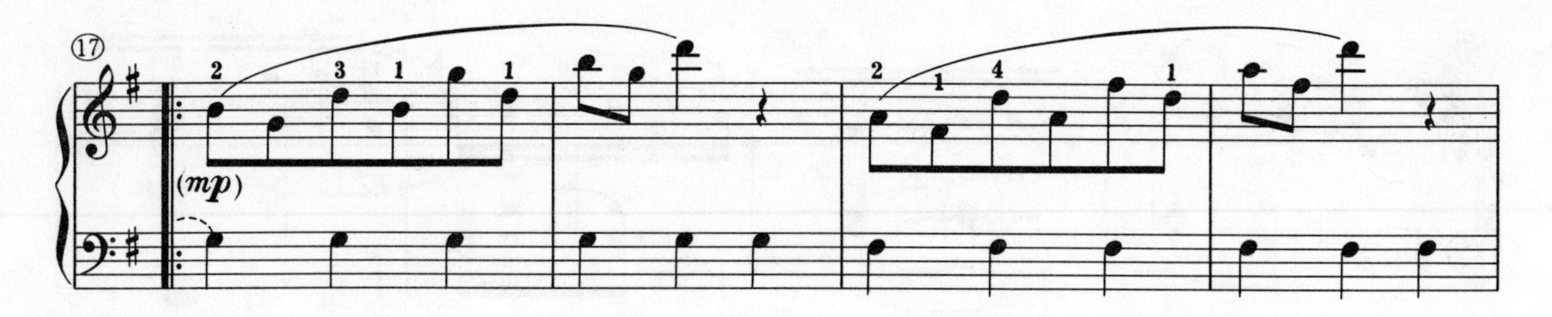
17
(mp)

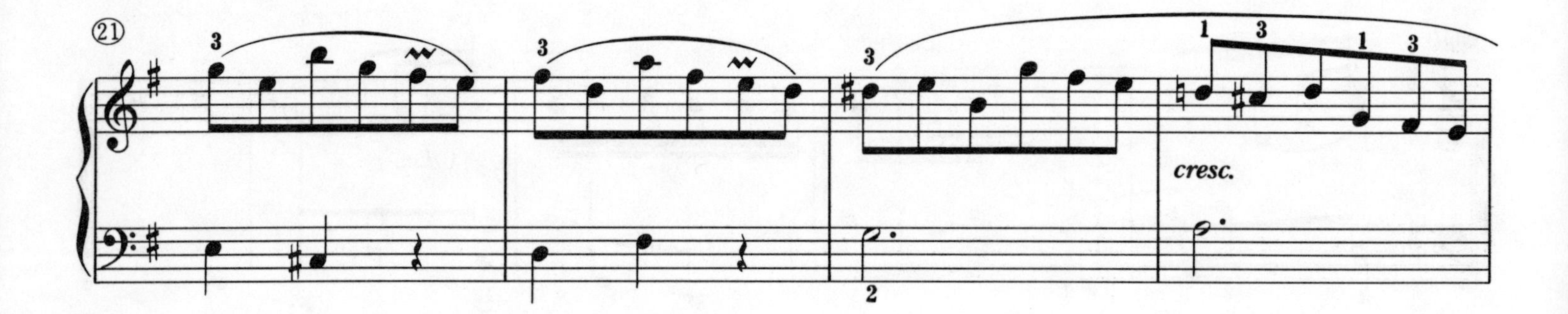
21
cresc.

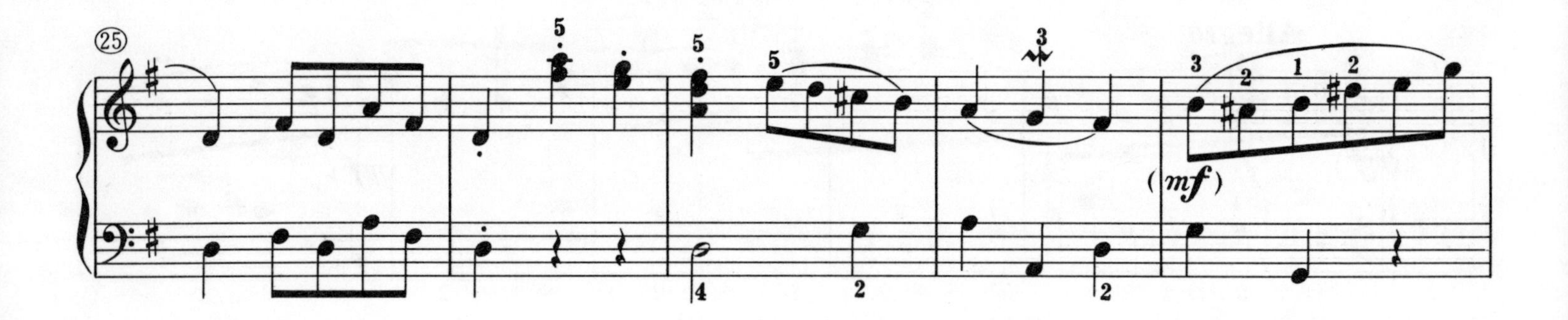
25
(mf)

30
p)

34

(mf)
(cresc.)

f

(mf)

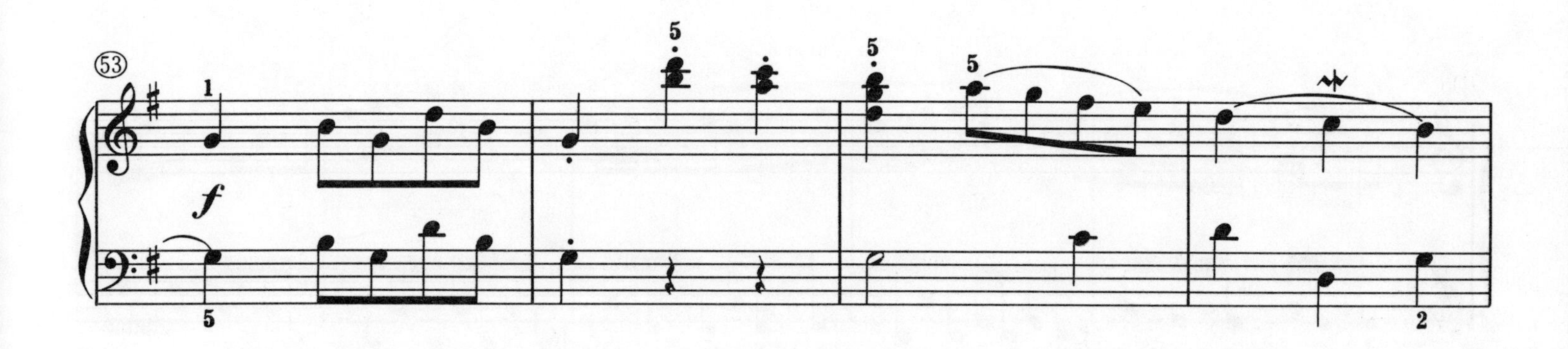
f

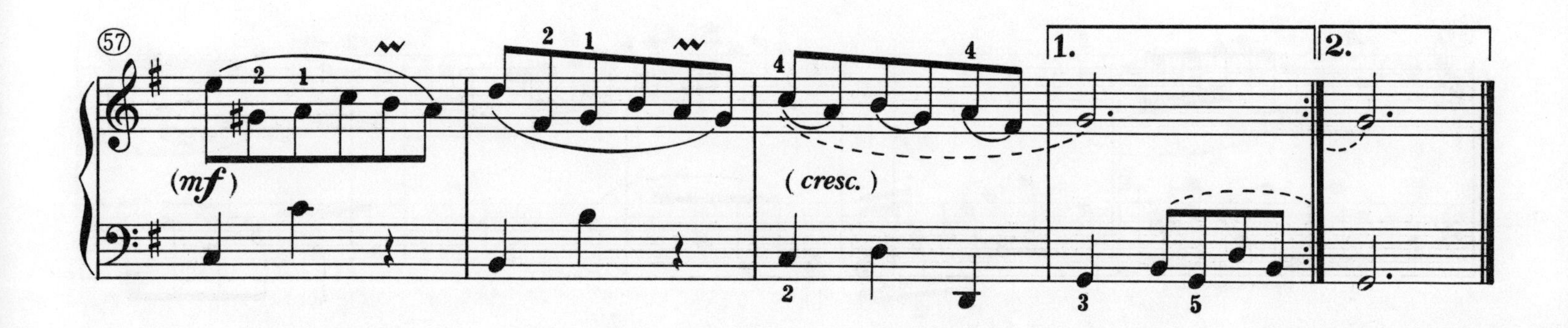
(mf)
(cresc.)
1.
2.

SONATA
Hob. XVI: 23

Joseph Haydn

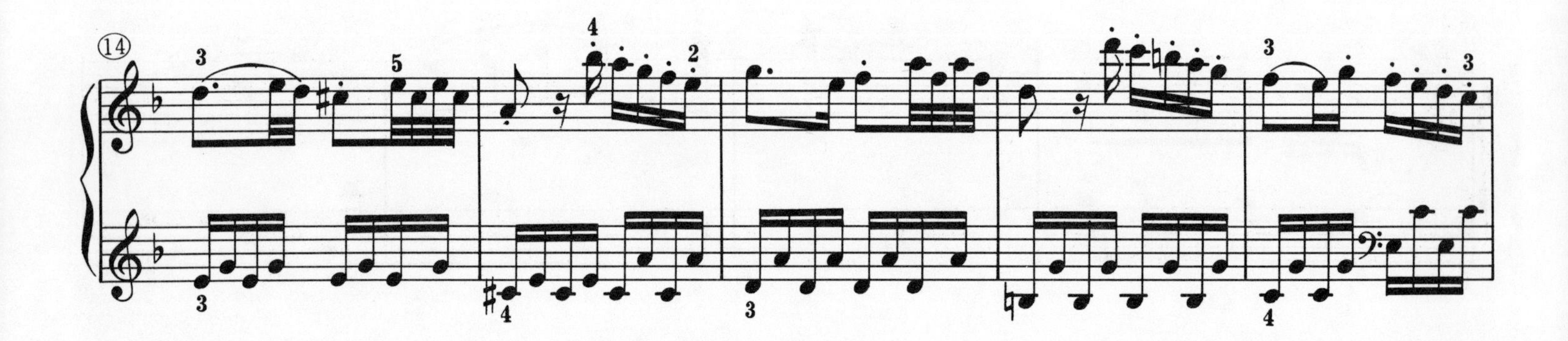

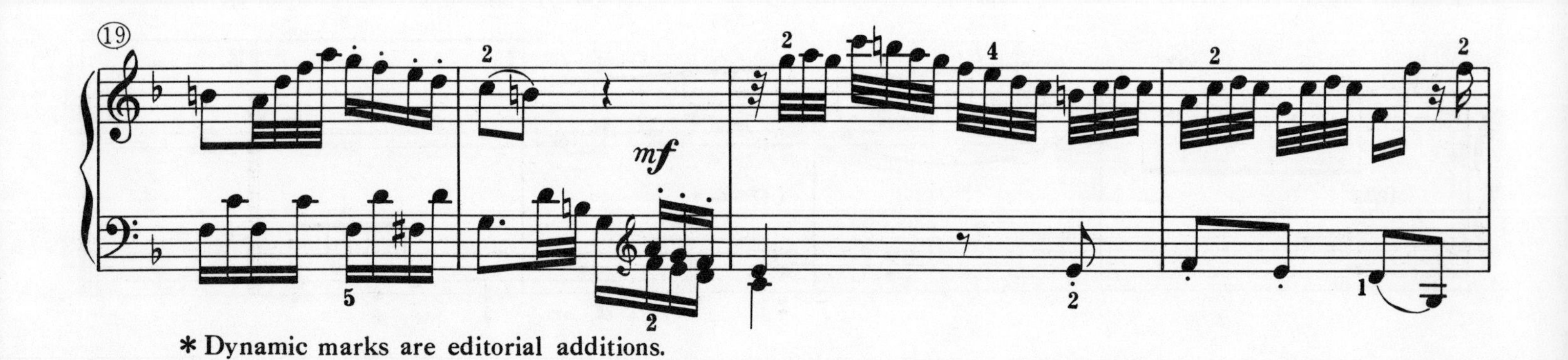

* Dynamic marks are editorial additions.

ten.

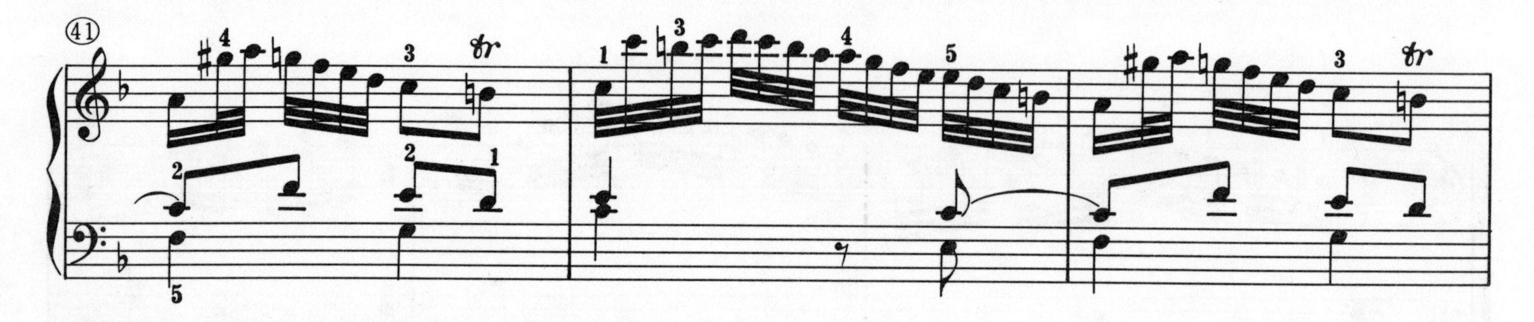

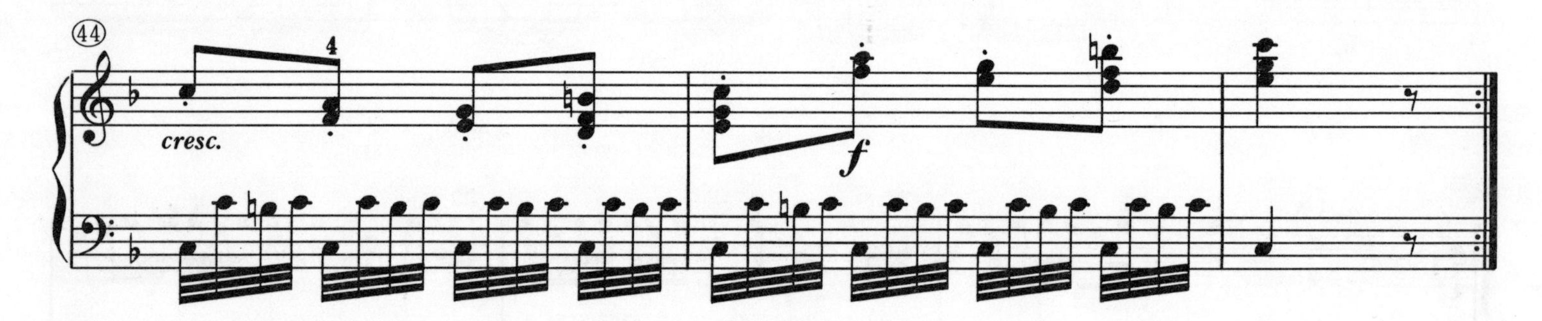
cresc.
f

p
mf

cresc.

f

p

cresc.

mf

cresc.

f

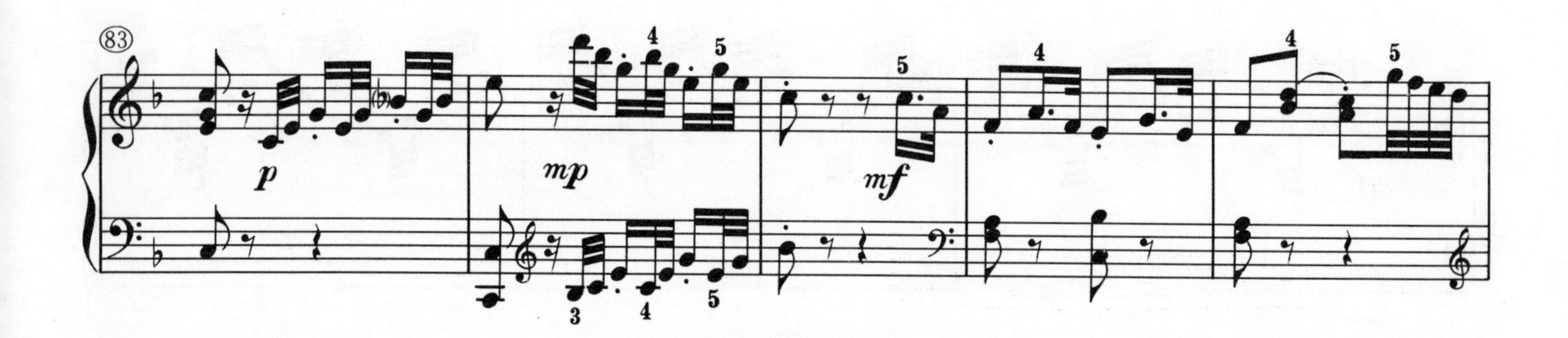
p
mp
mf

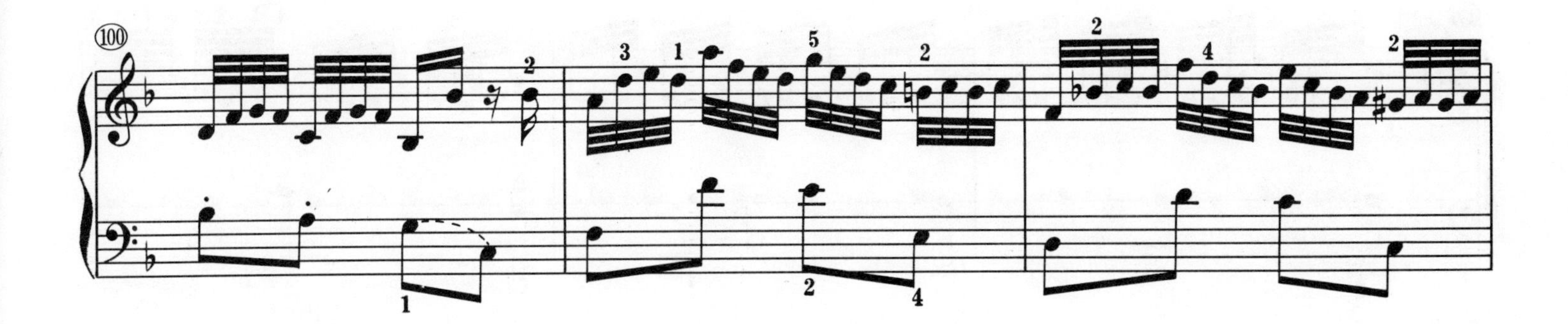

112

115

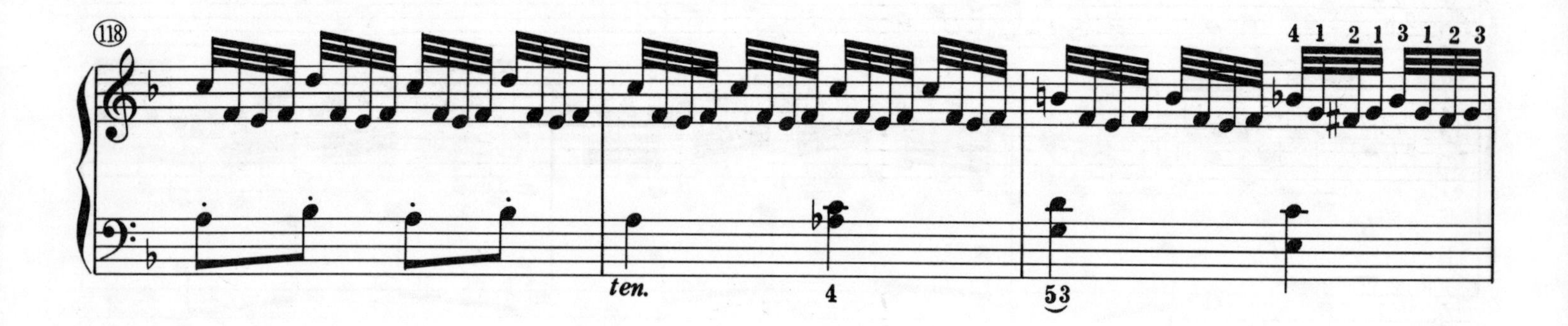
118
ten.

121

124
cresc.
f

Adagio

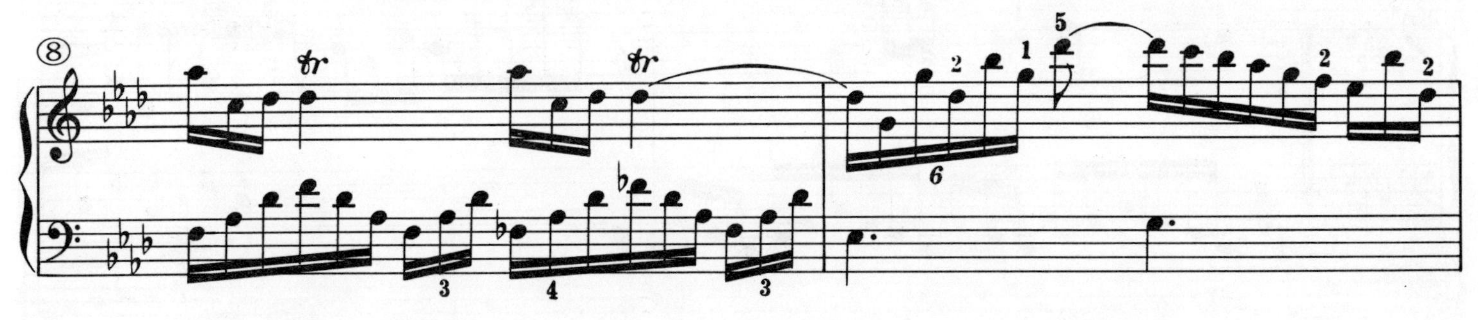

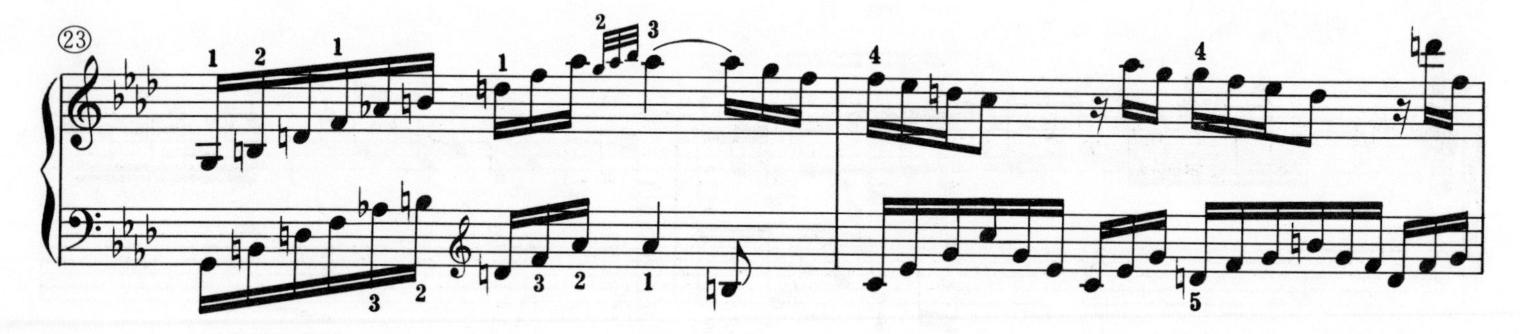

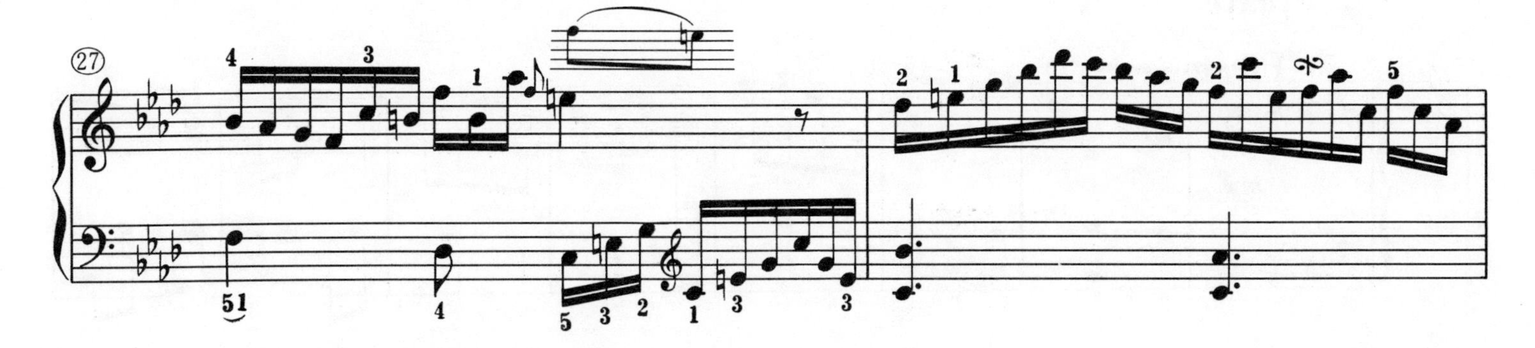

Finale

42

49
dim.
f

56
mf

63

70
cresc.
f

77

p

cresc.
mf

cresc.

f
dim.

mf

118
f

124
p
mp

130
cresc.
f
mp

136
mf
cresc.
f

142
dim.

SONATA

Domenico Cimarosa

Allegro alla francese

*Marks of articulation and dynamics are, for the most part, editorial additions.

18
p

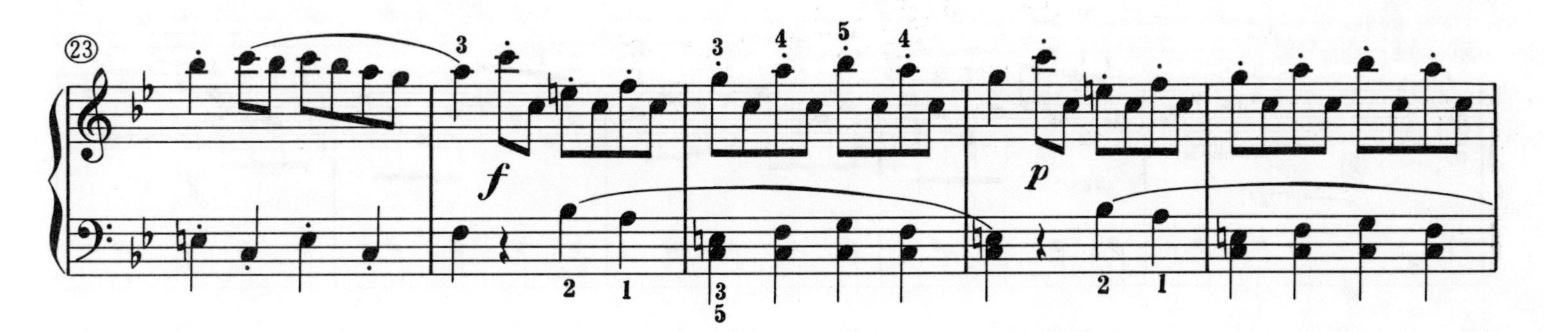
23
f
p

28
f
p

33
cresc.
f

38
p
p

43
f

cresc.

dim.

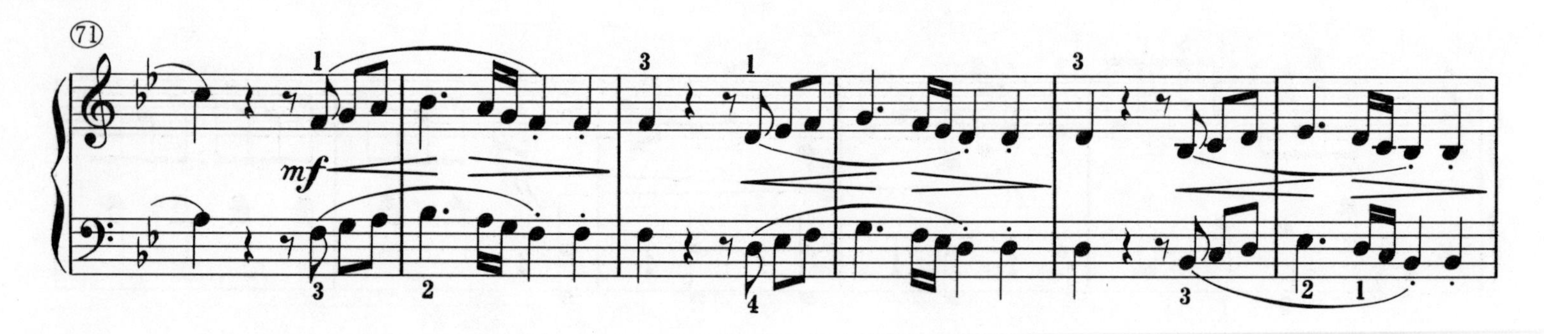

82
p

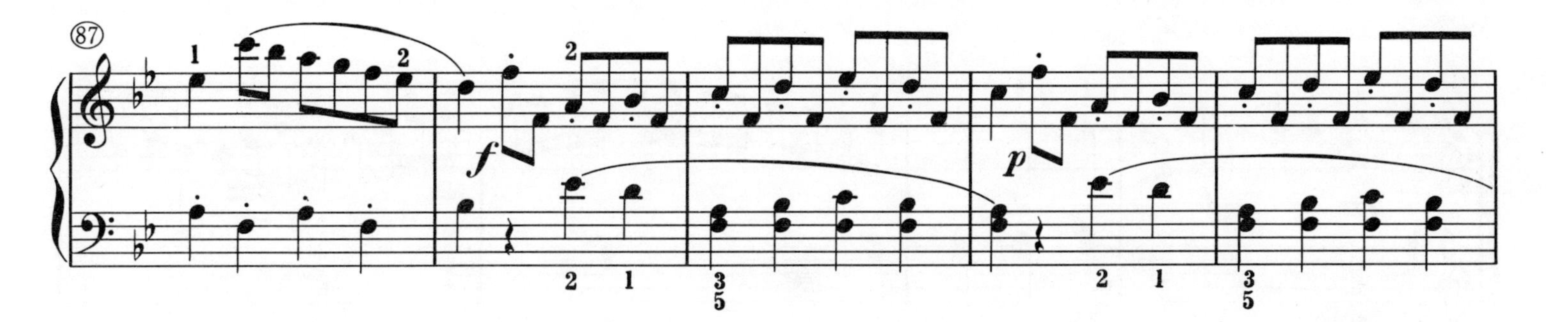
87
f
p

92
f

97
mp cresc.
f

102
p cresc.
f

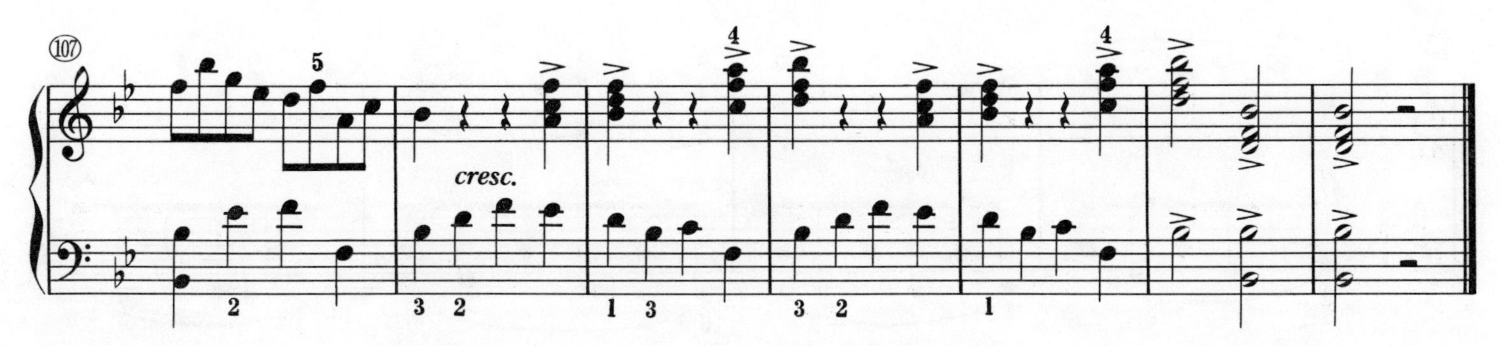
107
cresc.

SONATA

K. 283

Wolfgang Amadeus Mozart

Allegro

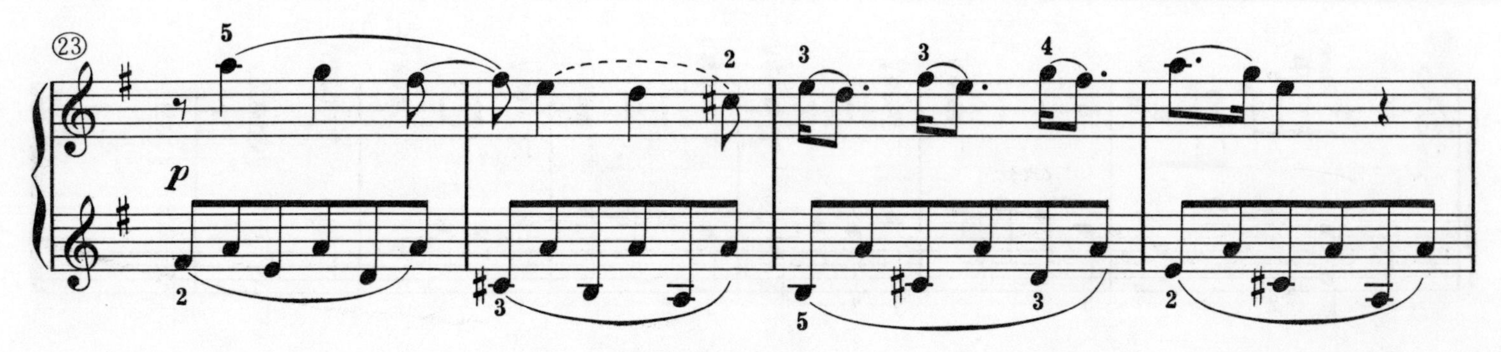

m. d.
m. s.

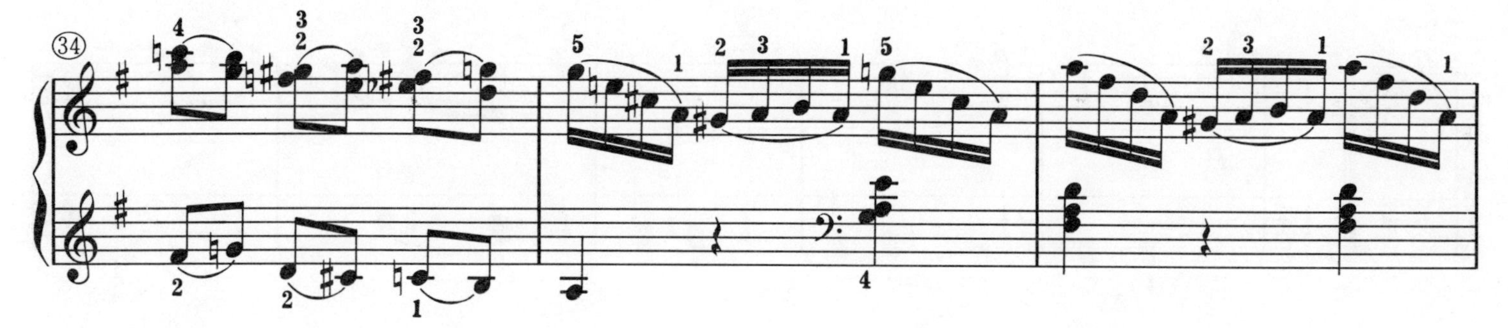

tr
tr

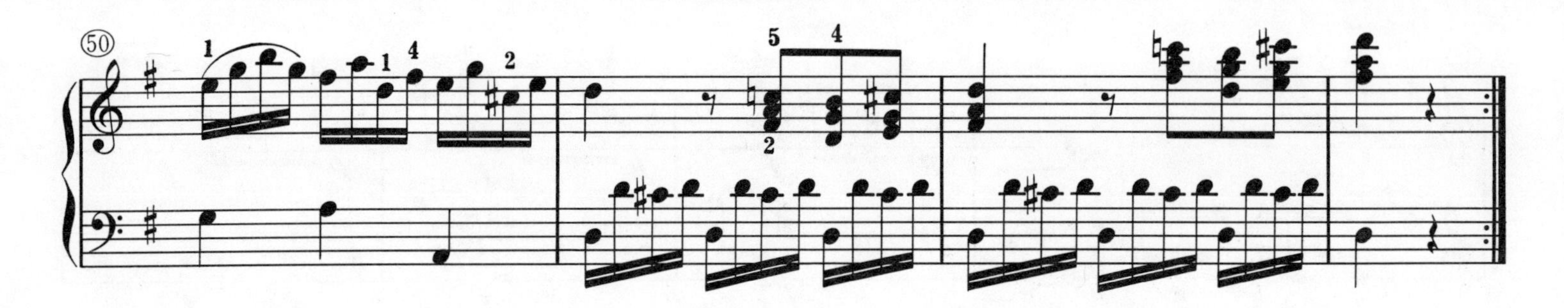

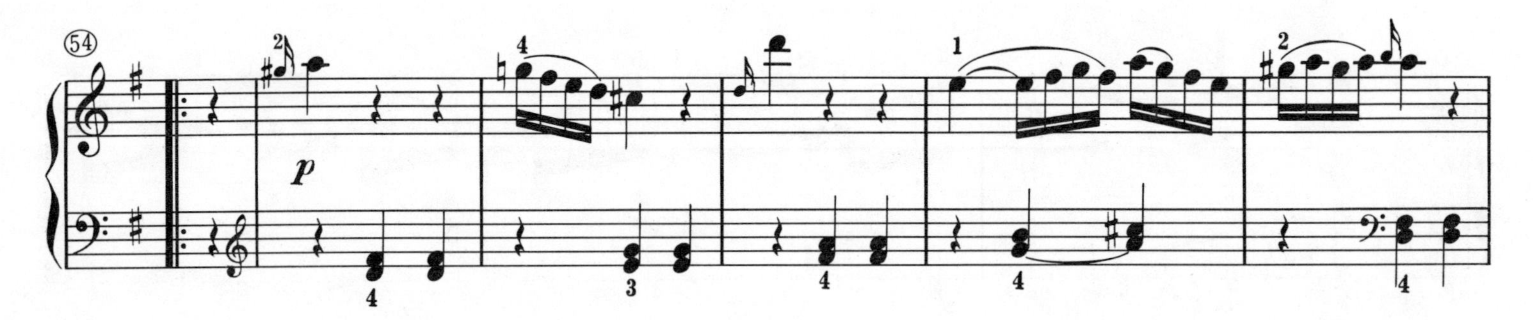

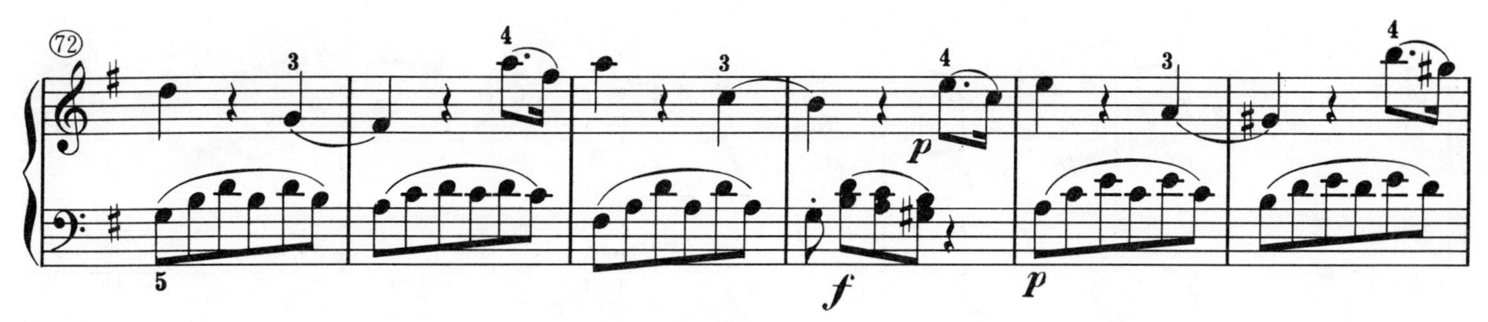

tr

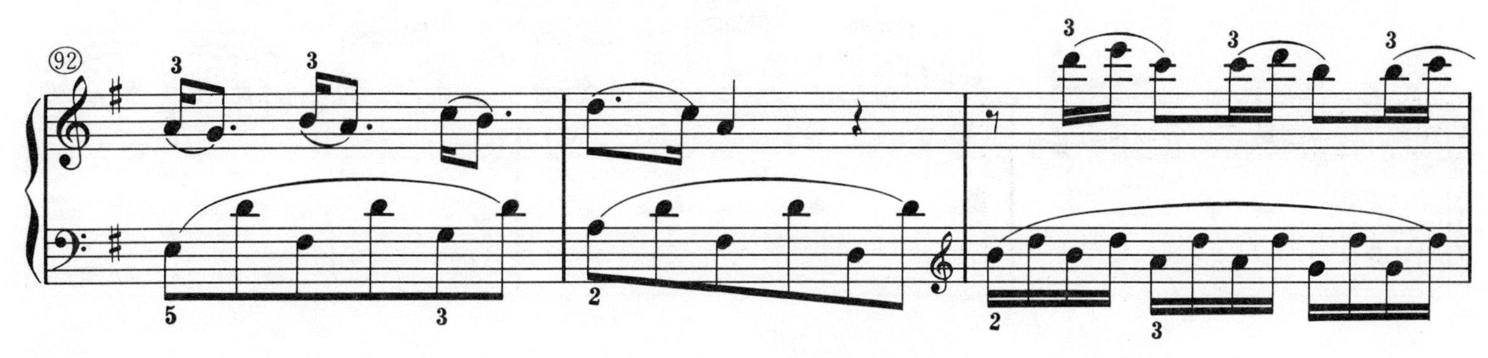

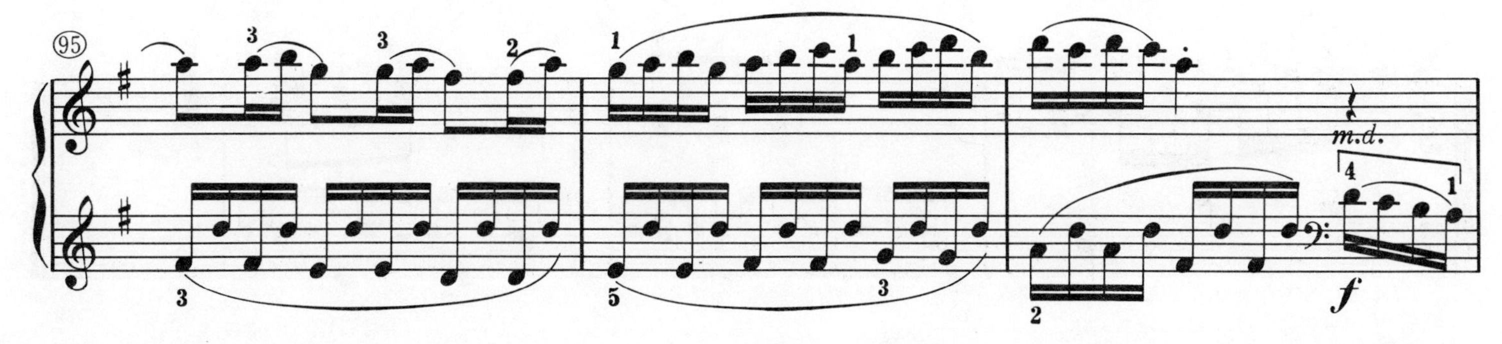
m.d.

98
m.s.

103

107

110

114

117

Andante
p

f

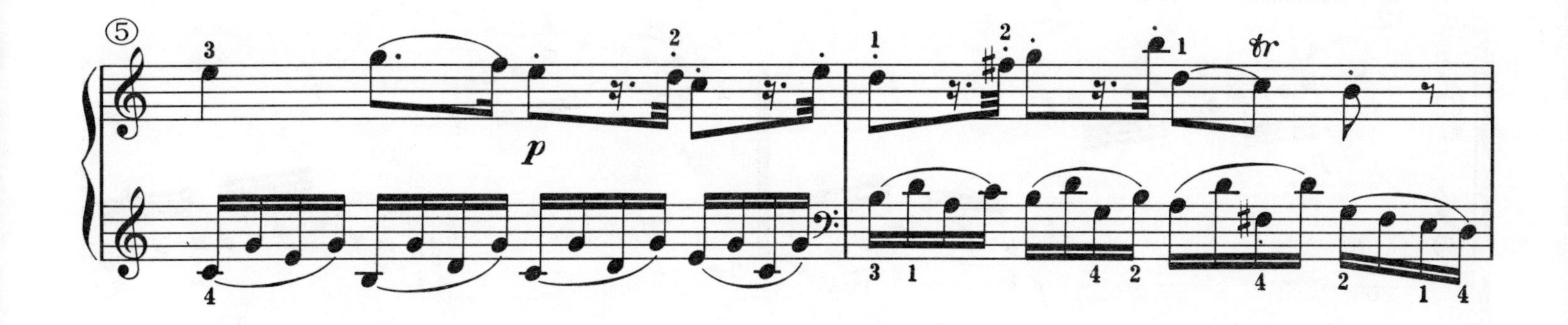
p

f
decresc.
p

f
p

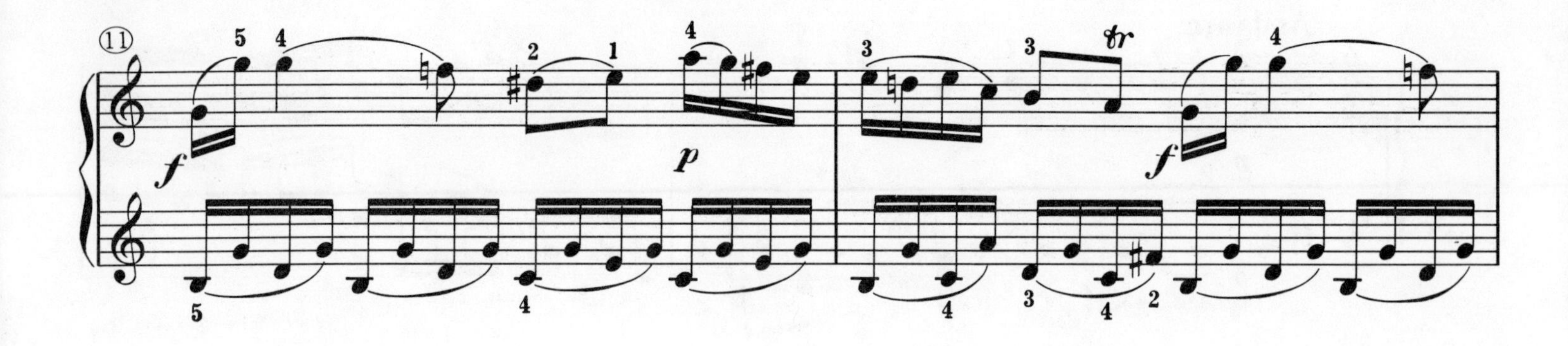

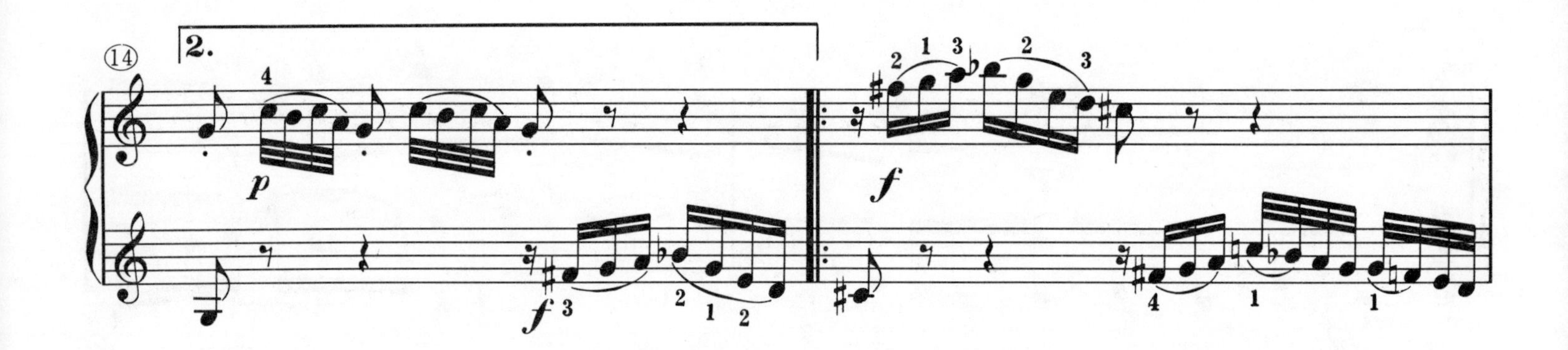

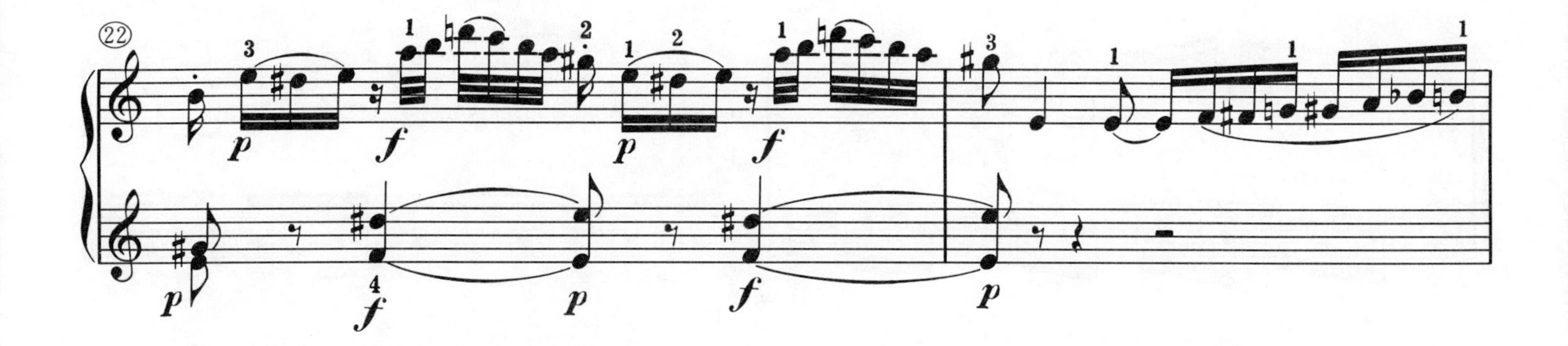

decresc.

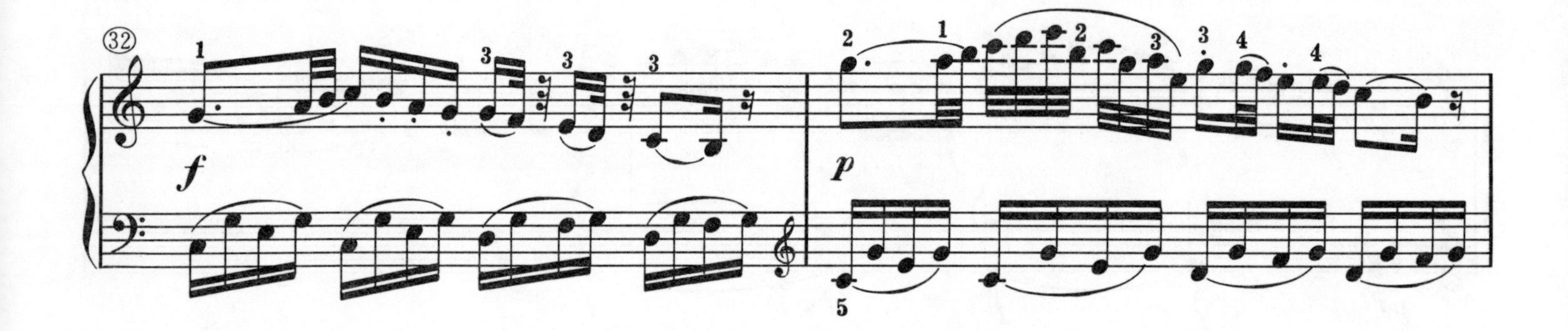

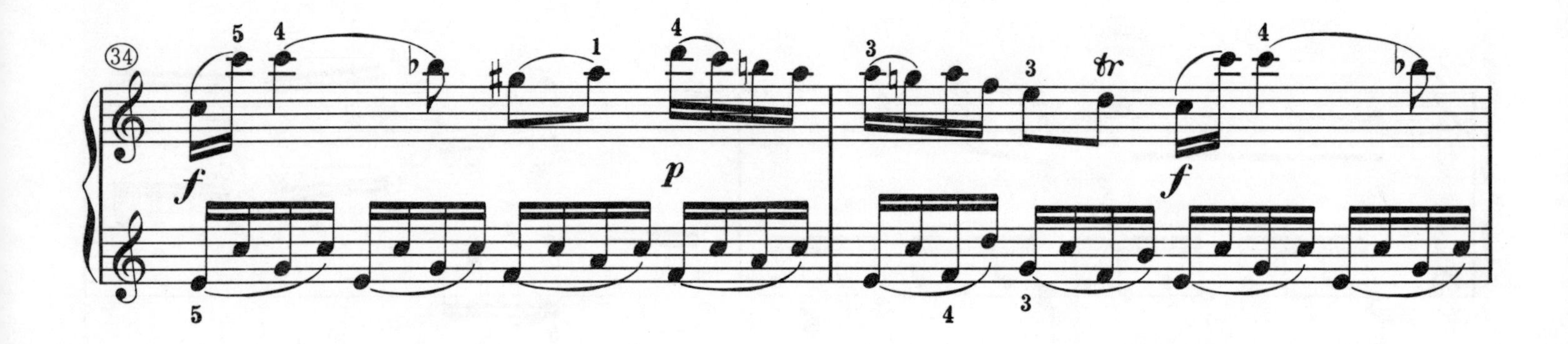

1.

2.

Presto
(mp)

(cresc.)
(f)

p

f

p

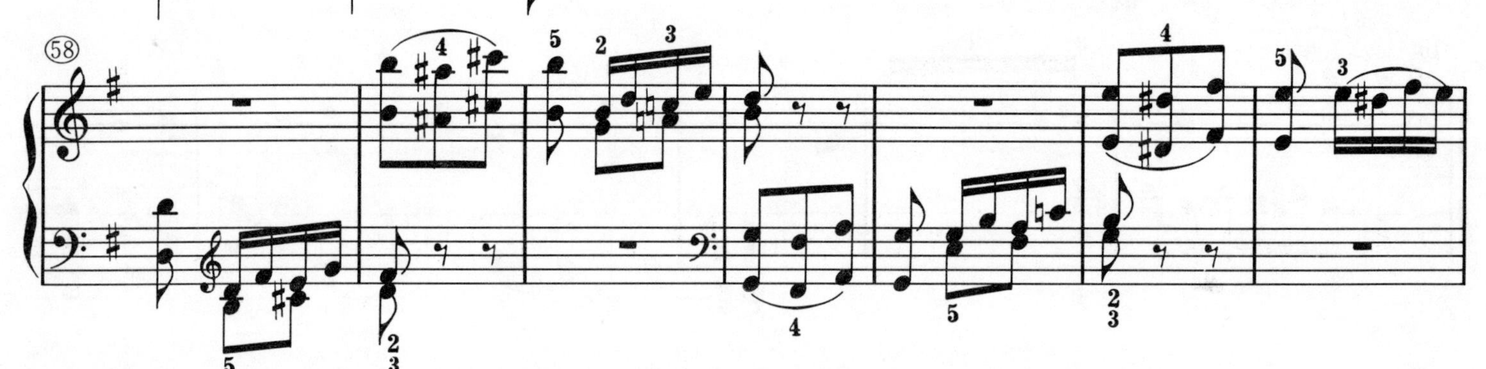

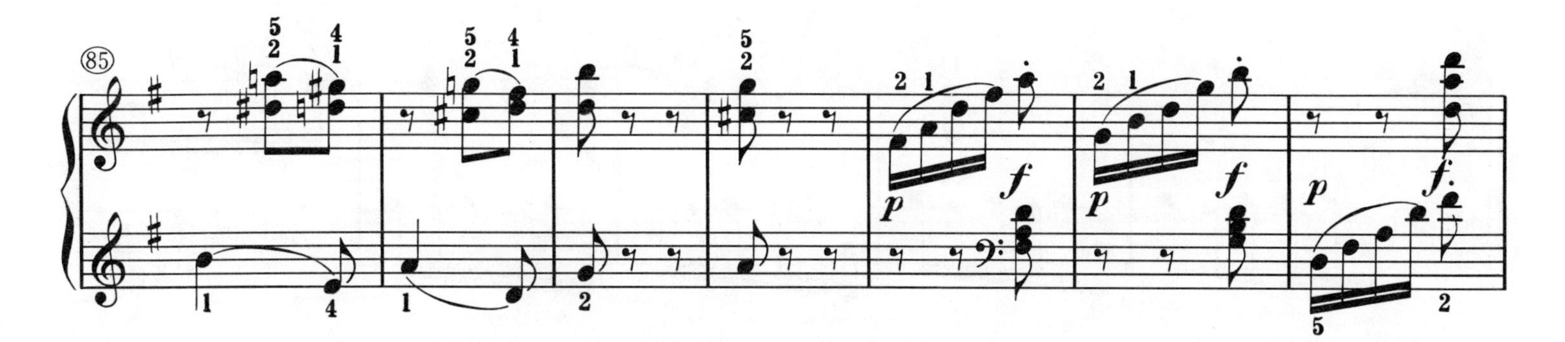

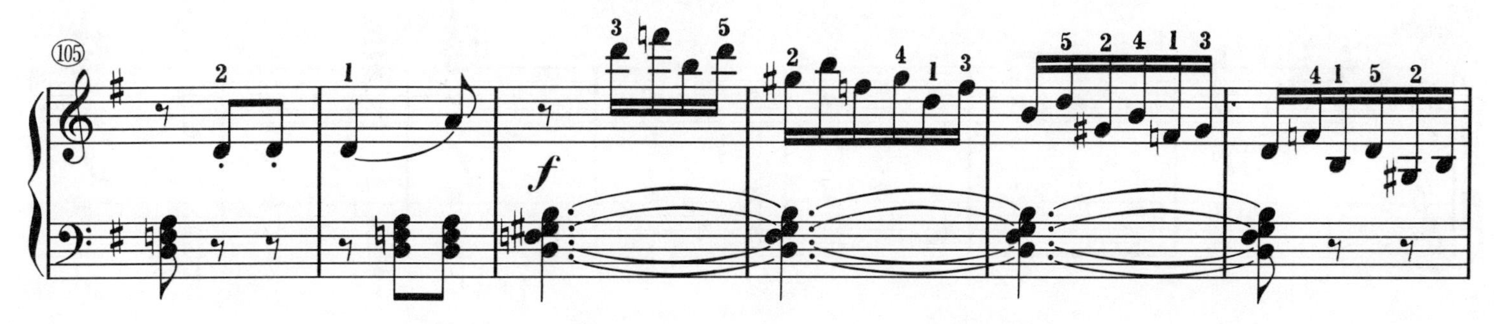

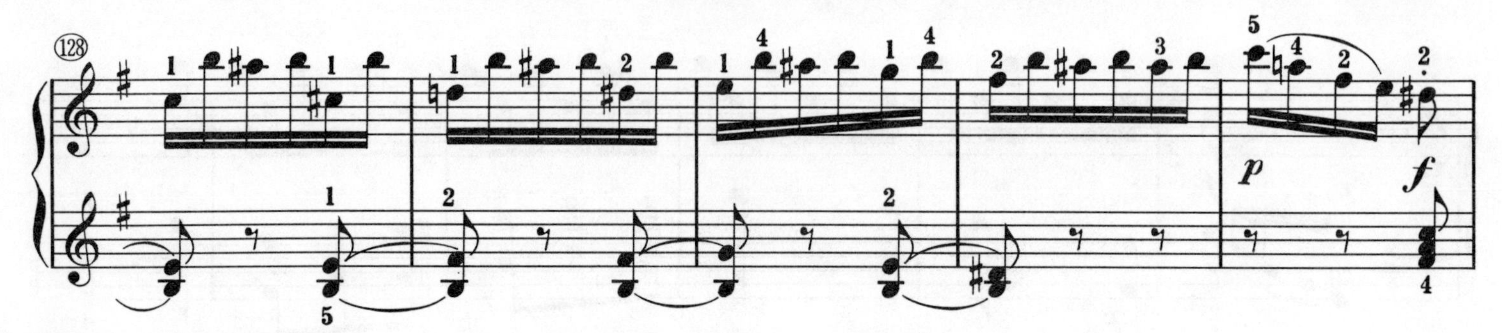

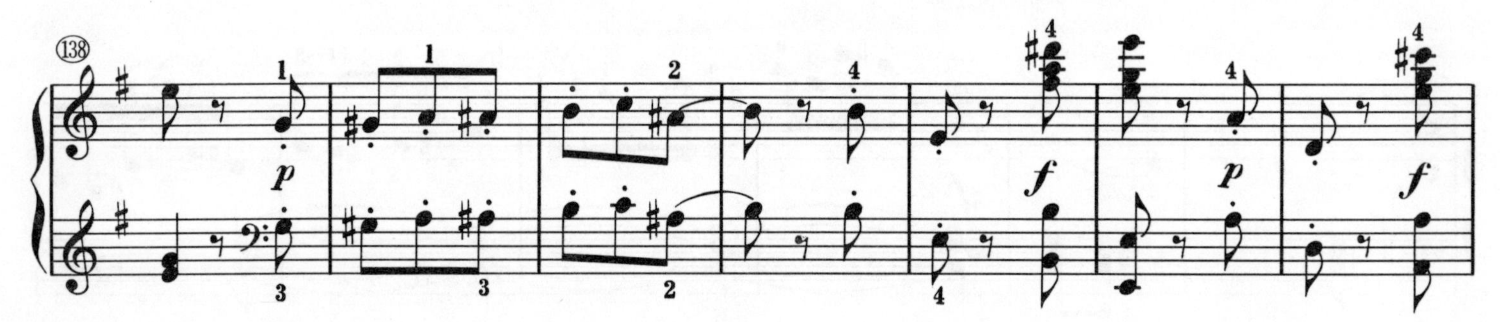

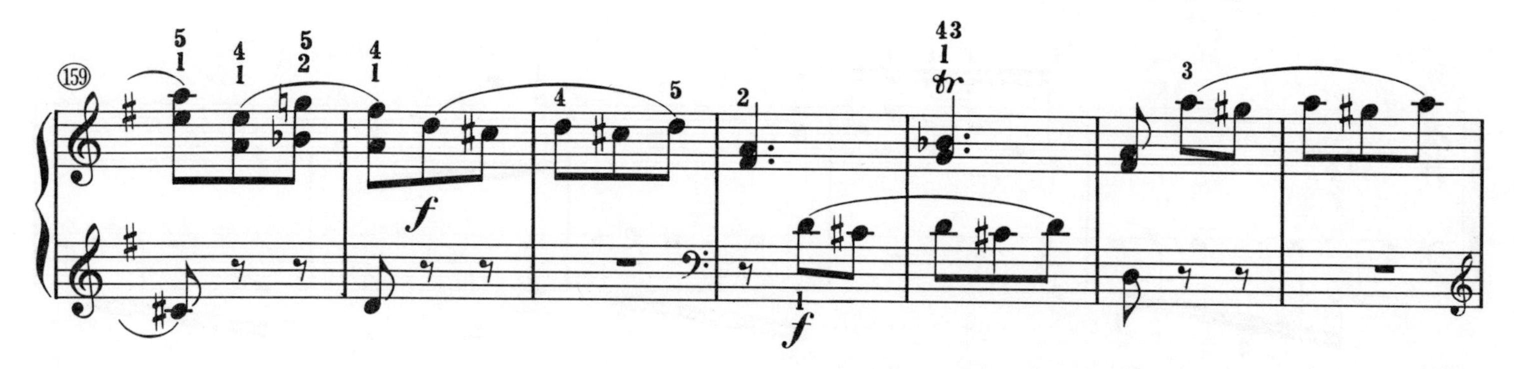
159

166

172
(mp)

179
(cresc.)

184

189

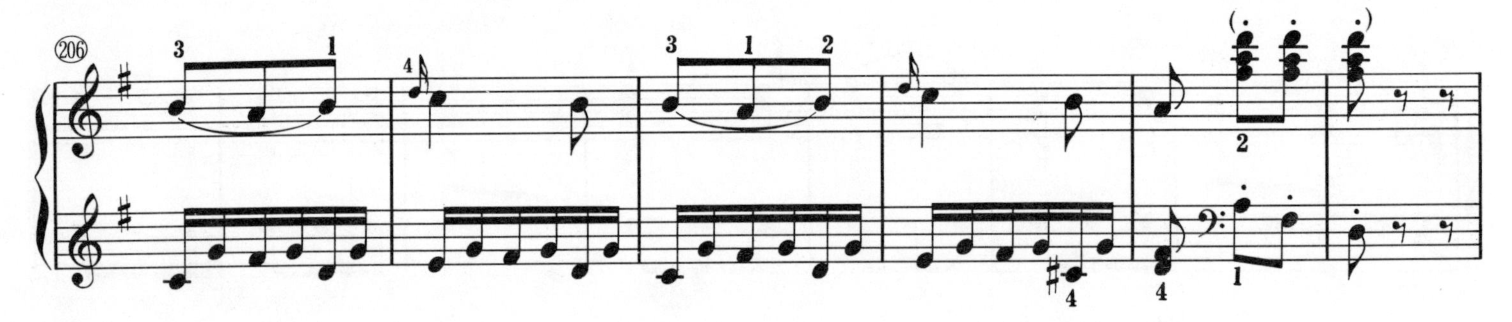

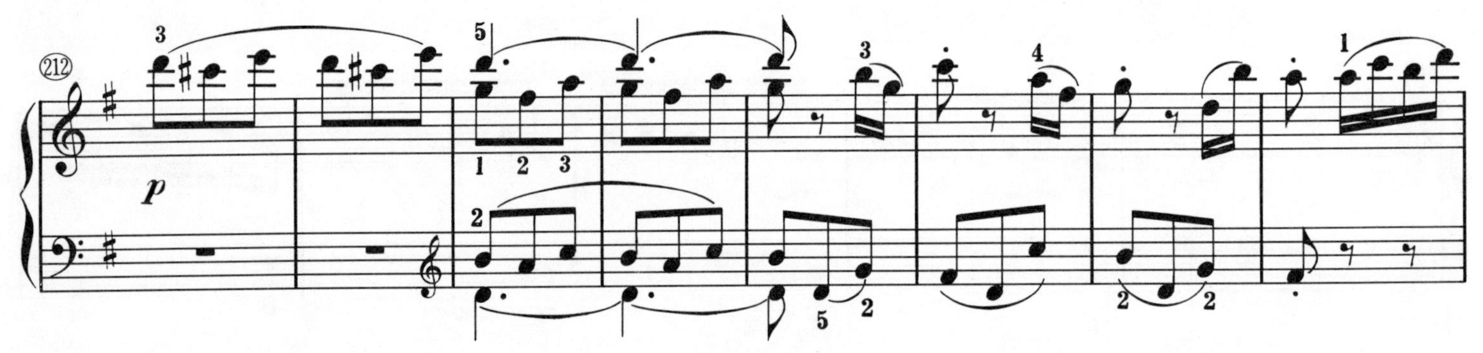

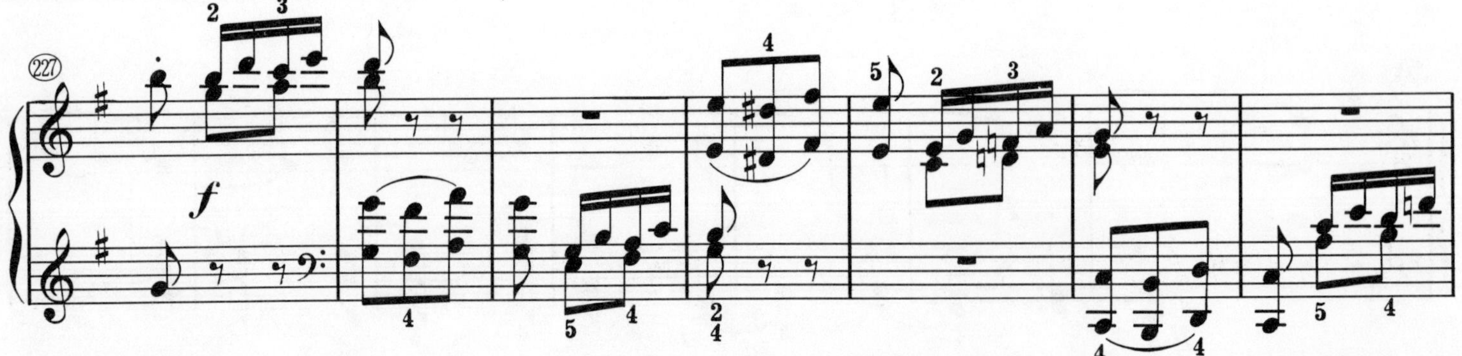

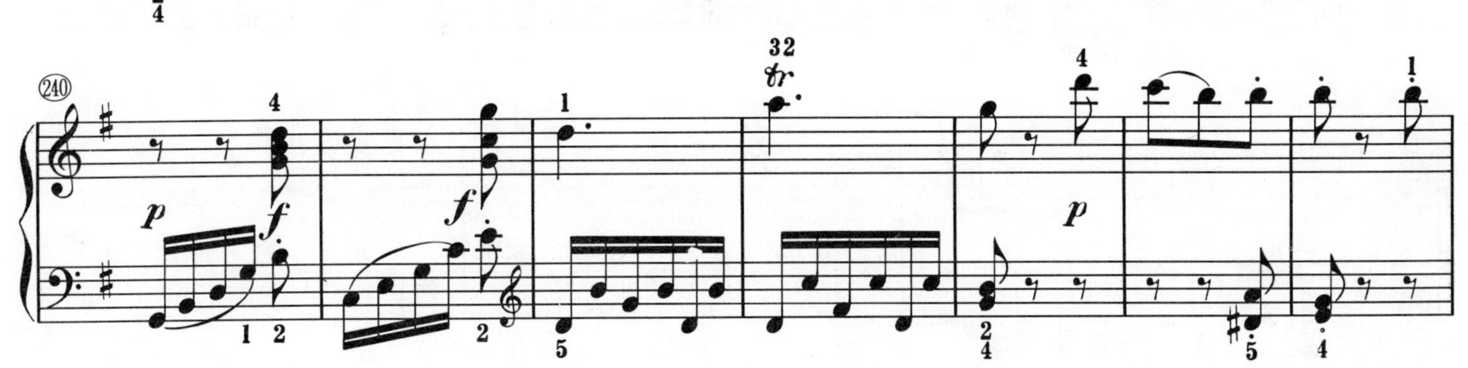

Coda

SONATA

Op. 26, No. 3

Muzio Clementi

*Clementi's *Presto* marks, in general, can not be interpreted literally and are closer to today's *Allegro*. In most cases they indicate a fast four-to-a-measure beat and not an *Alla breve*.

20
più f

23
p
sf
p

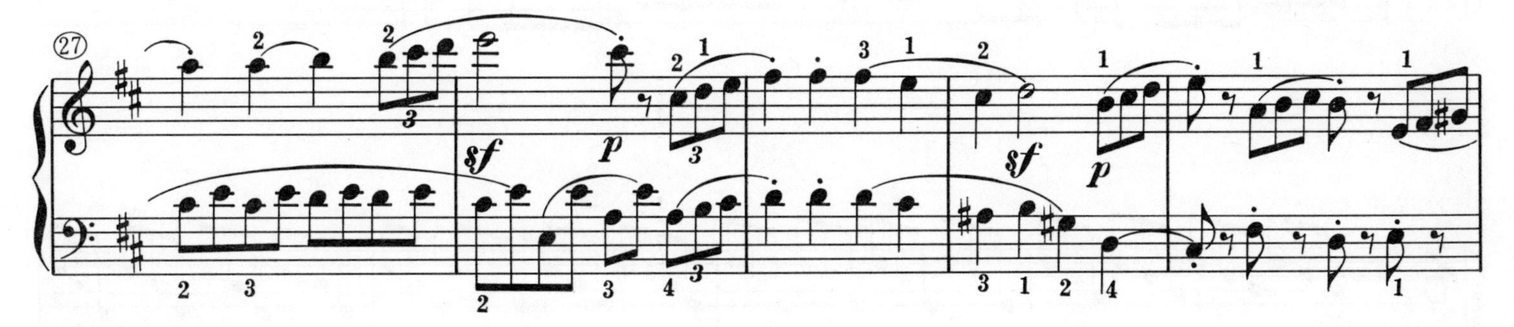

27
sf
p
sf
p

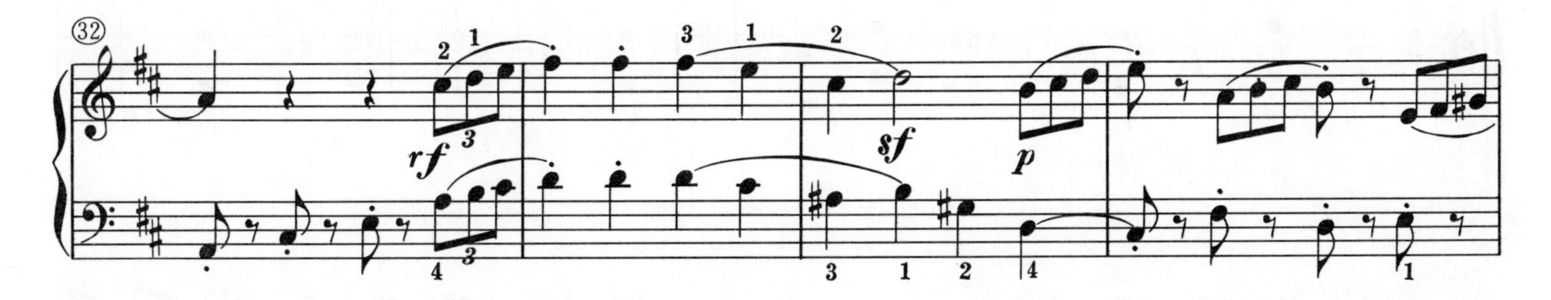

32
rf
sf
p

36
f

39
sf
sf
p
pp
sf
p
pp

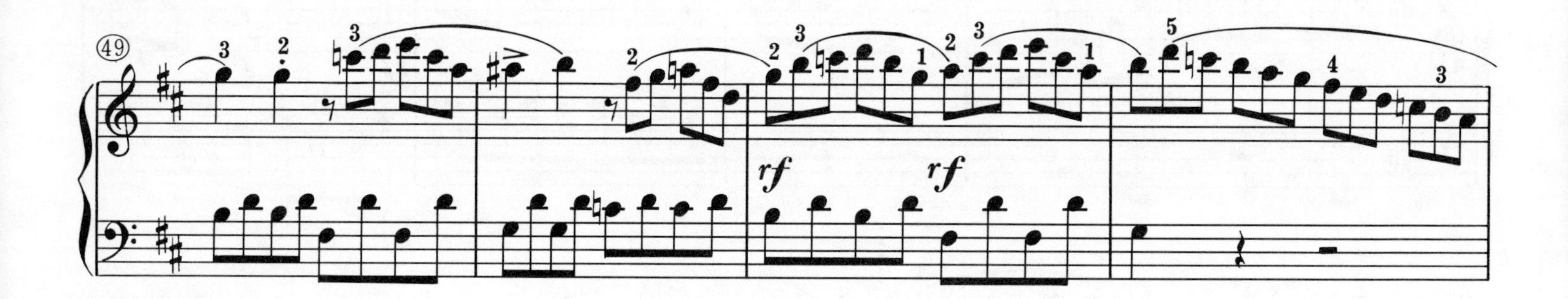
49

53

57

61
dim.

65
dimin.
pp
f
sf
sf
p

70
mf
(legato sempre)

74
pp
cresc.

77
p
p

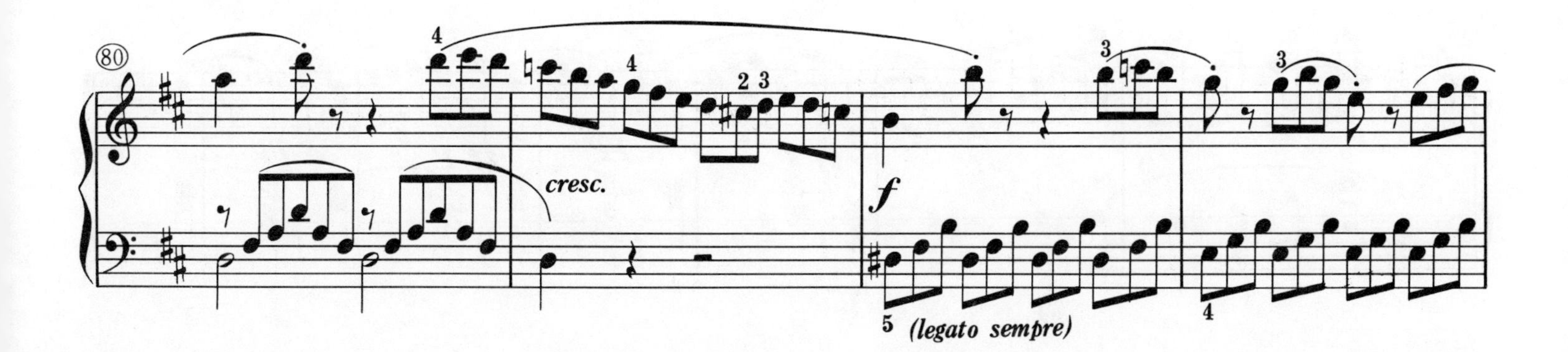
80
cresc.
f
(legato sempre)

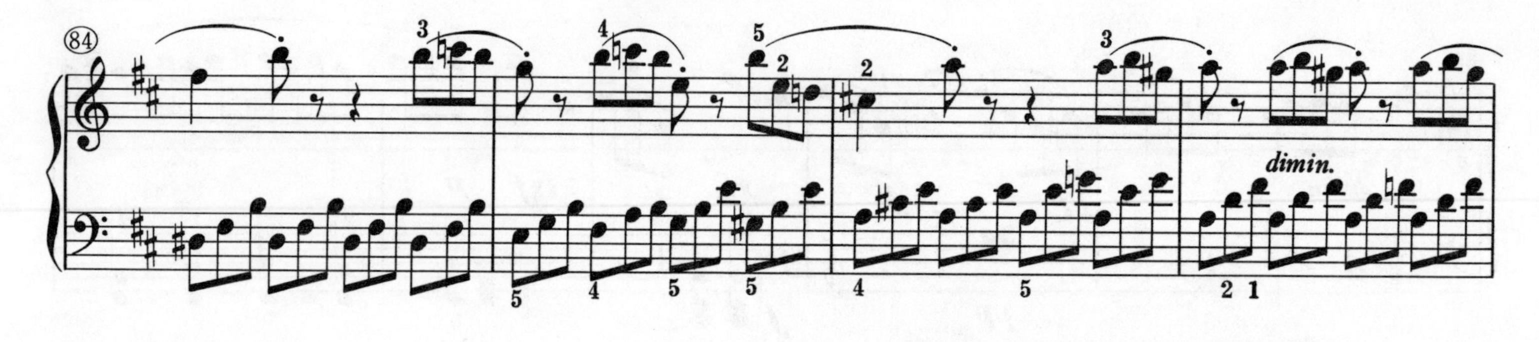
dimin.

p
cresc.

f
p
p

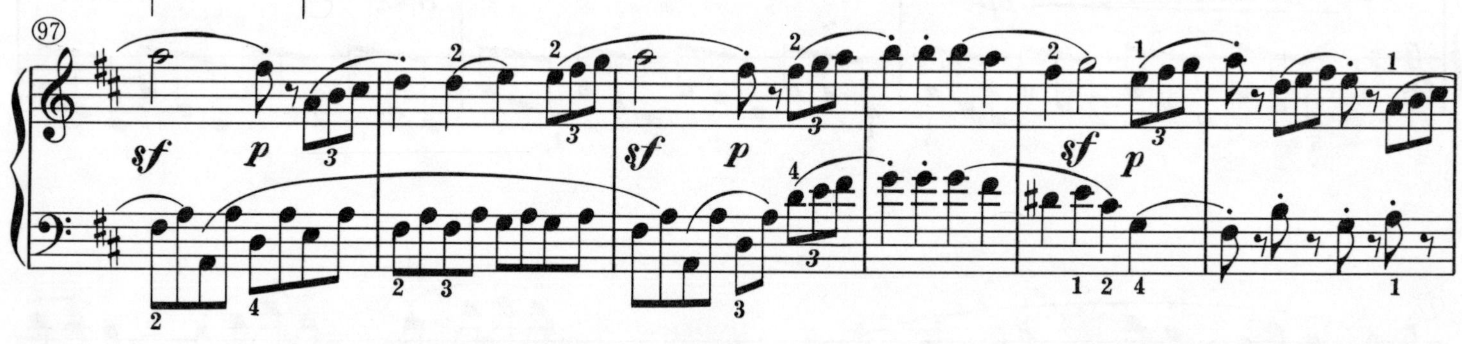
sf
p
sf
p
sf
p

rf
sf
p
f

sf
sf p
pp
sf p
pp

Un poco andante

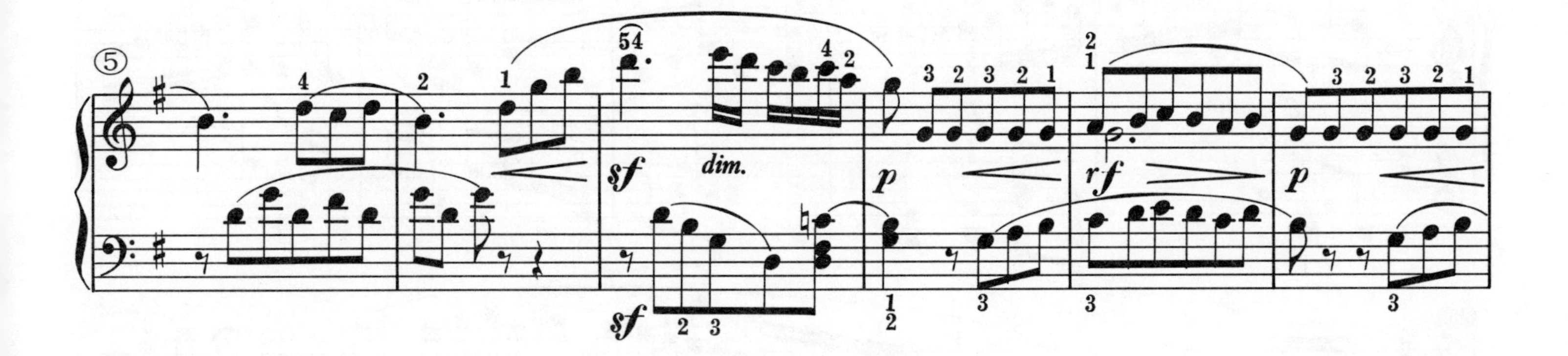

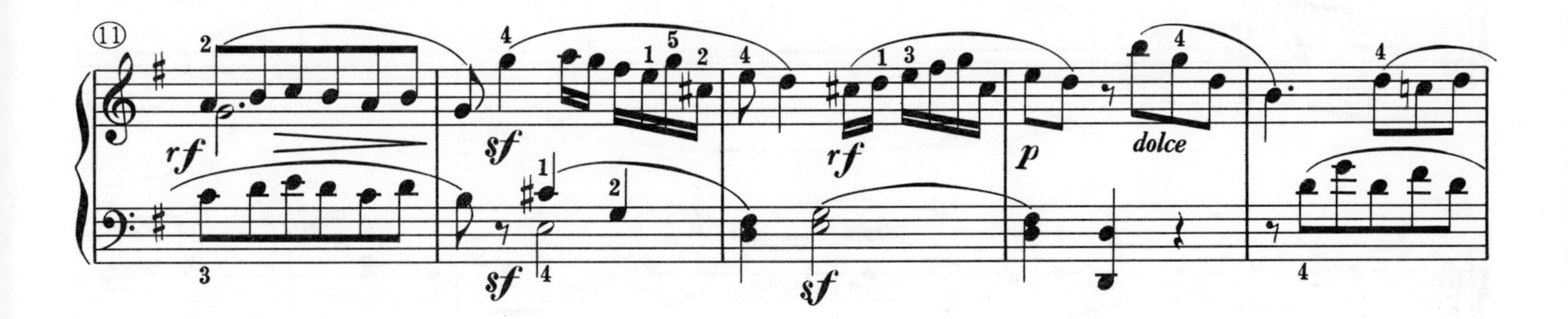

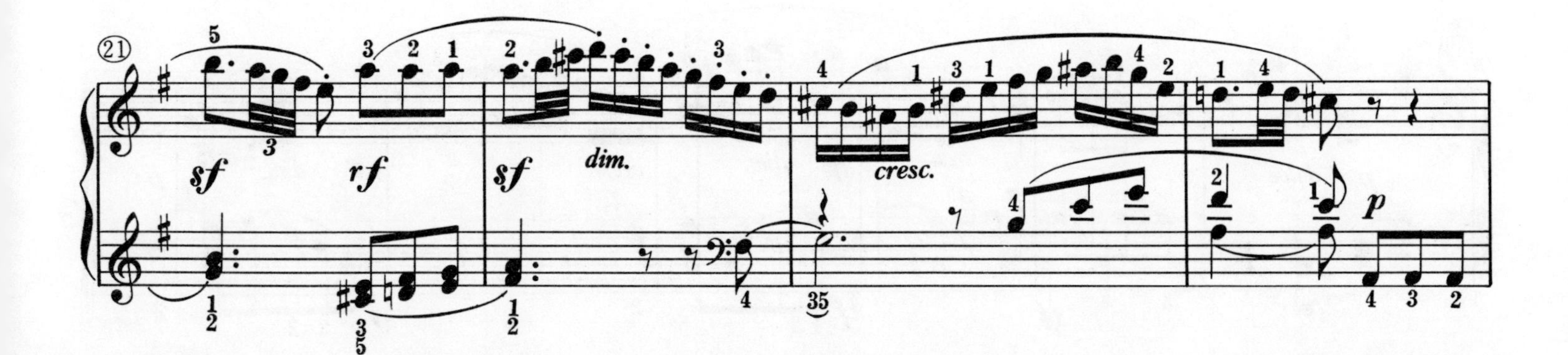

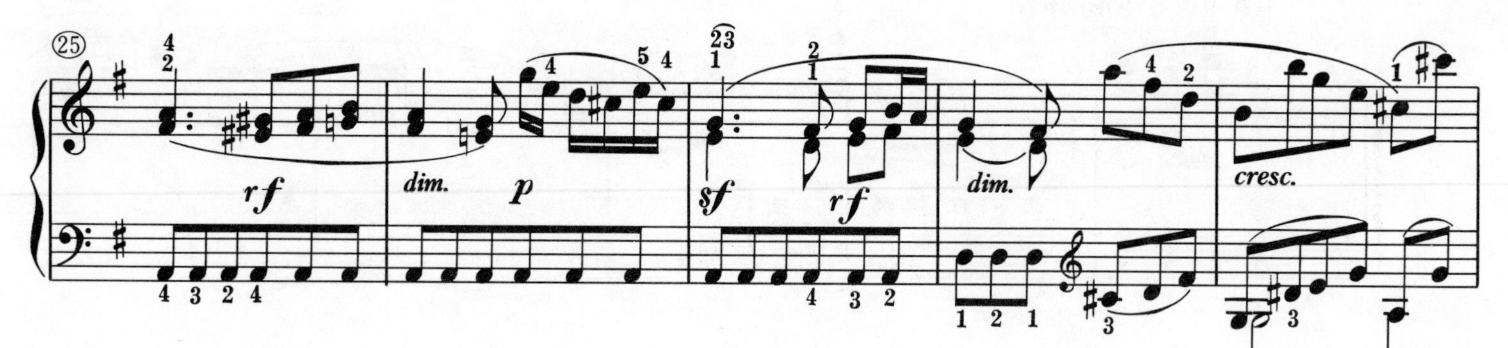
25
rf
dim.
p
sf
rf
dim.
cresc.

30
f
dim.
p
cresc.
f
dim.

35
p
cresc.
dim.
dolce

39
sf
p
rf
sf
dim.
sf

46
p
rf
p
rf
sf
rf
sf
sf

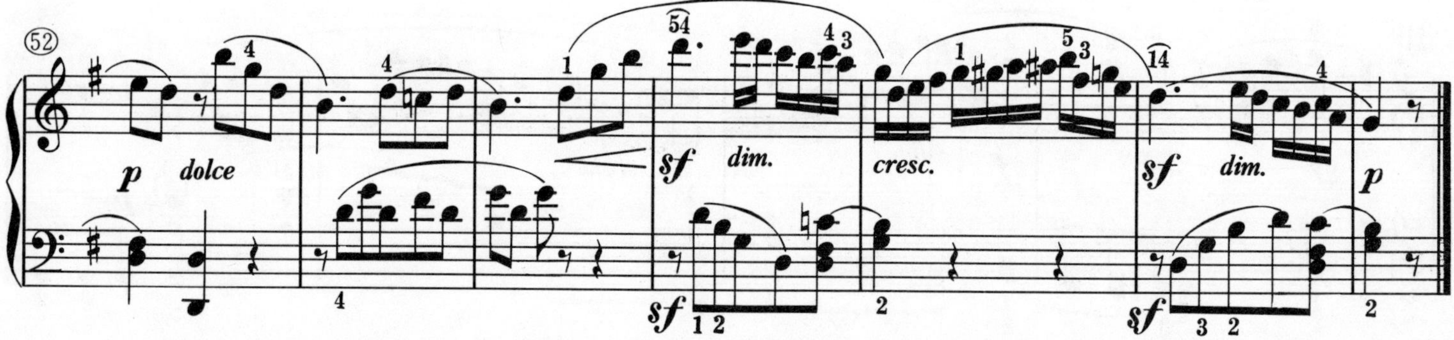
52
p
dolce
sf
dim.
cresc.
sf
dim.
p
sf
sf

Rondo

Assai allegro

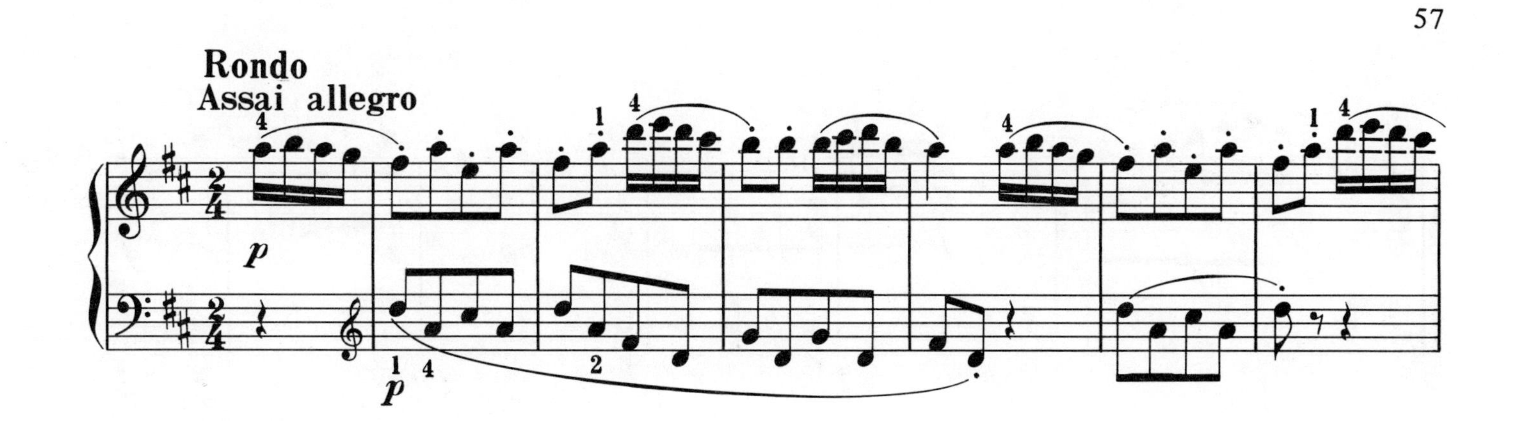

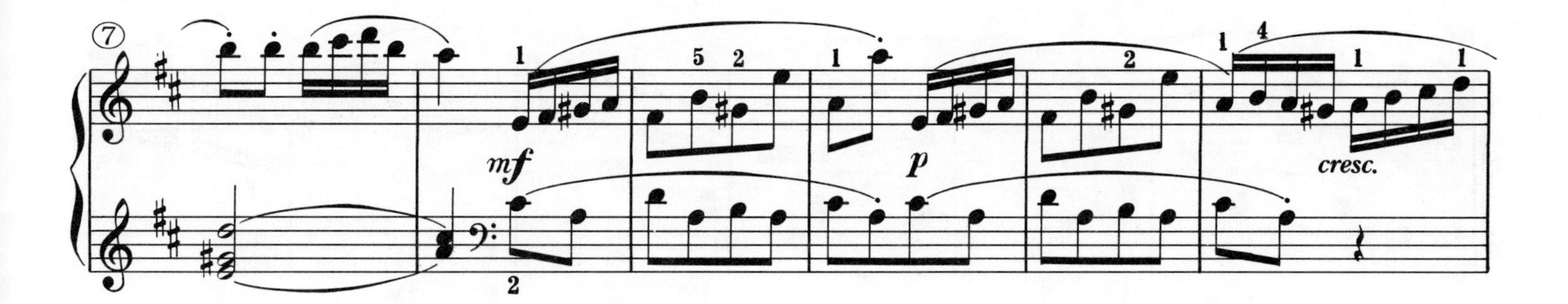

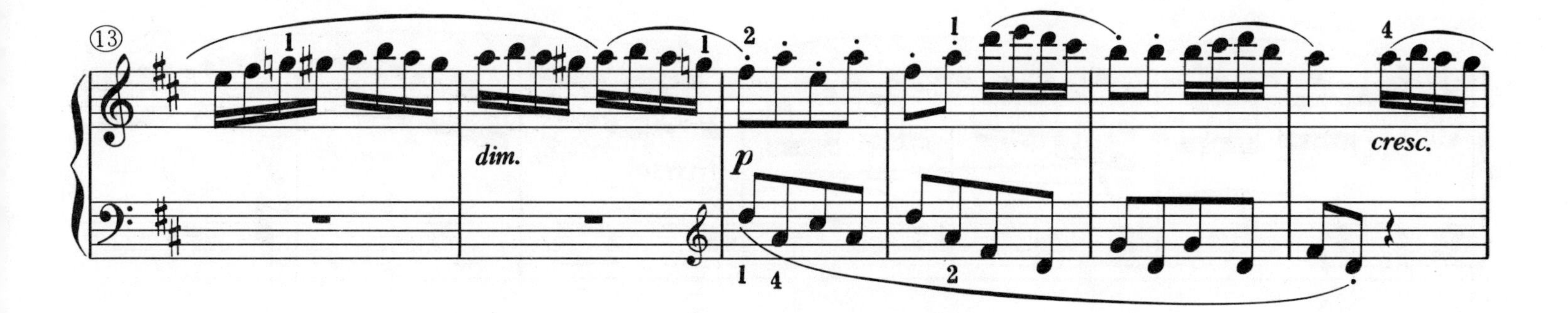

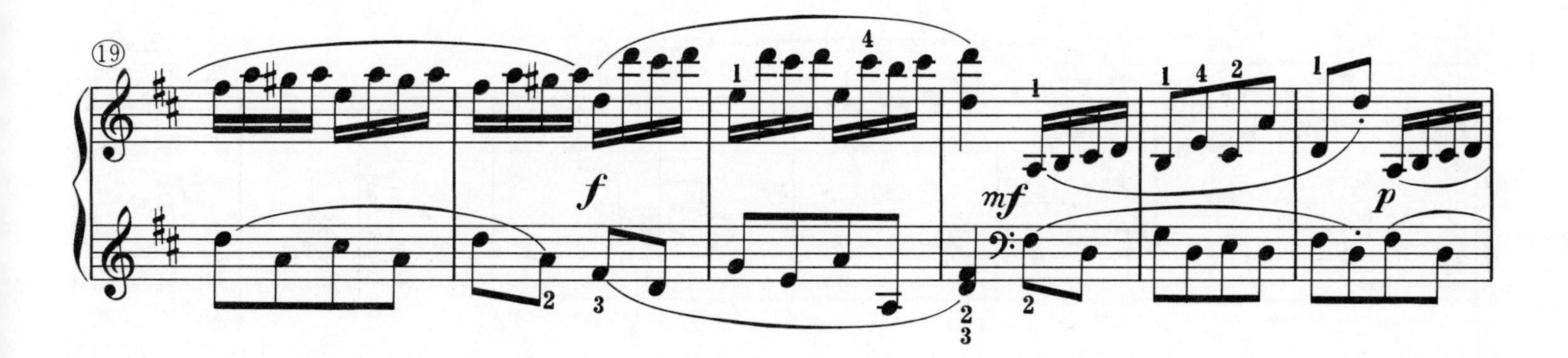

p cresc.

rall.
a tempo
cresc.

p (legato)

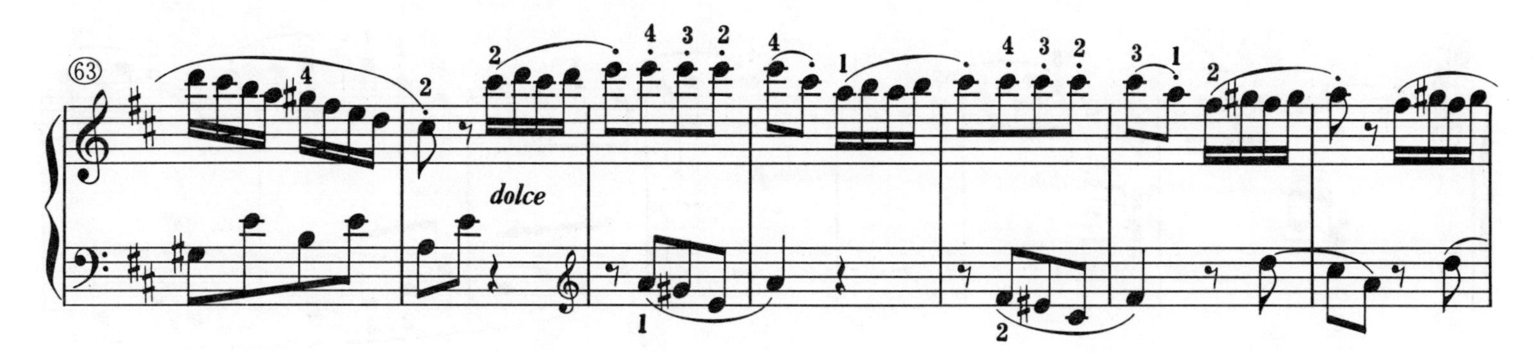
63
dolce

70
rf
rf
f
f

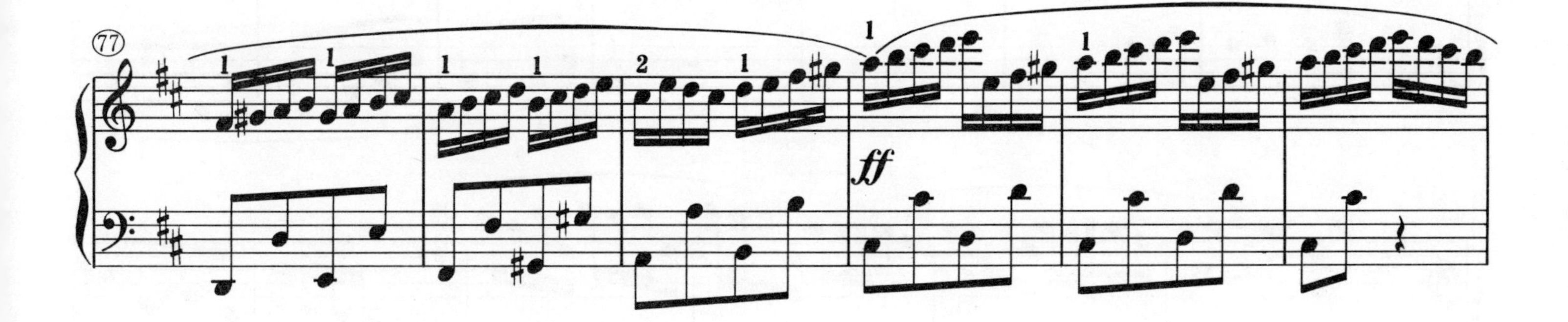
77
ff

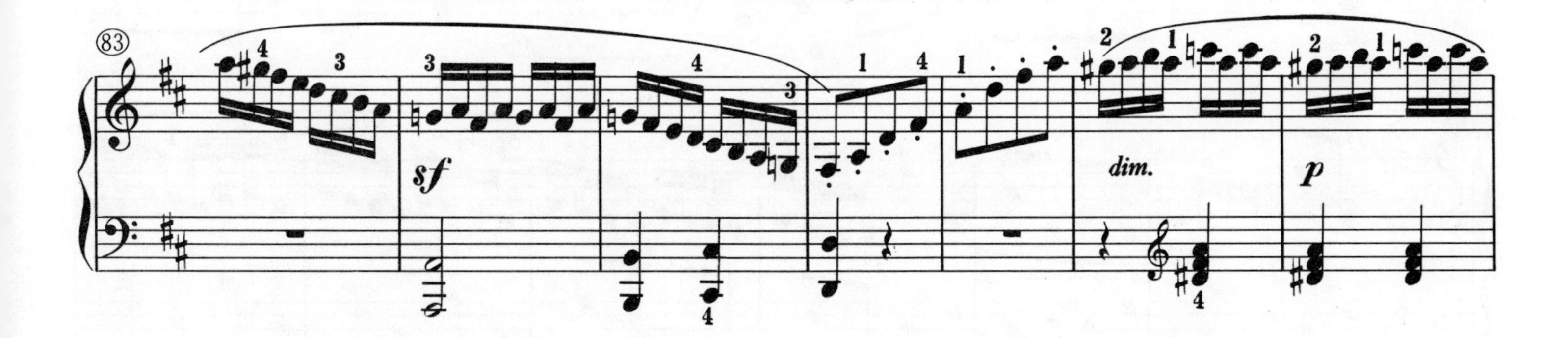
83
sf
dim.
p

90
f

97
dim.

104

111
cresc.
dim.

118
cresc.

124

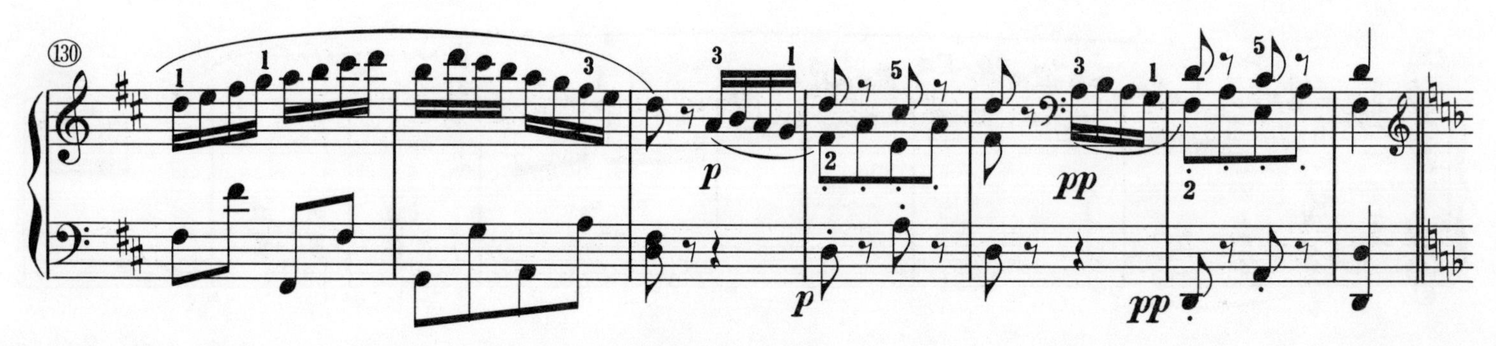
130

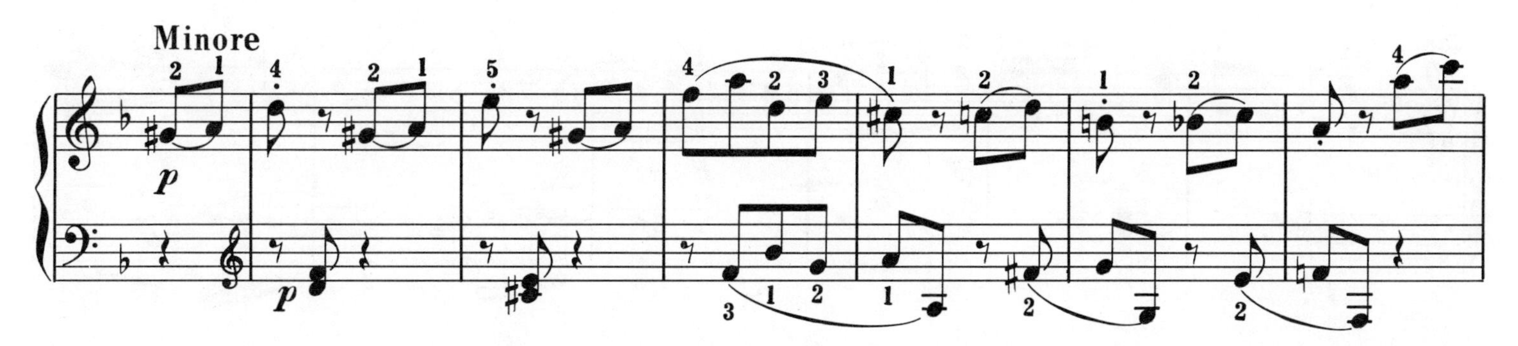
Minore
p
p

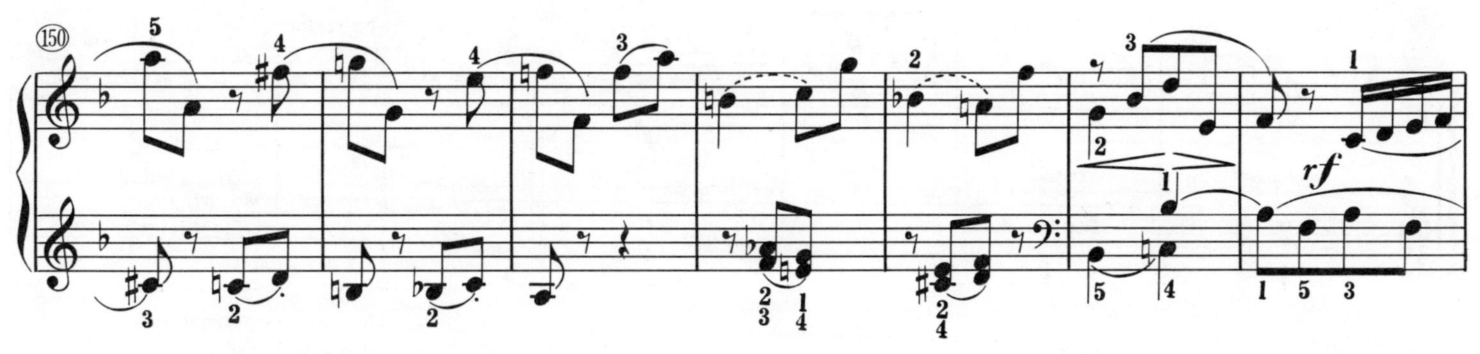
rf

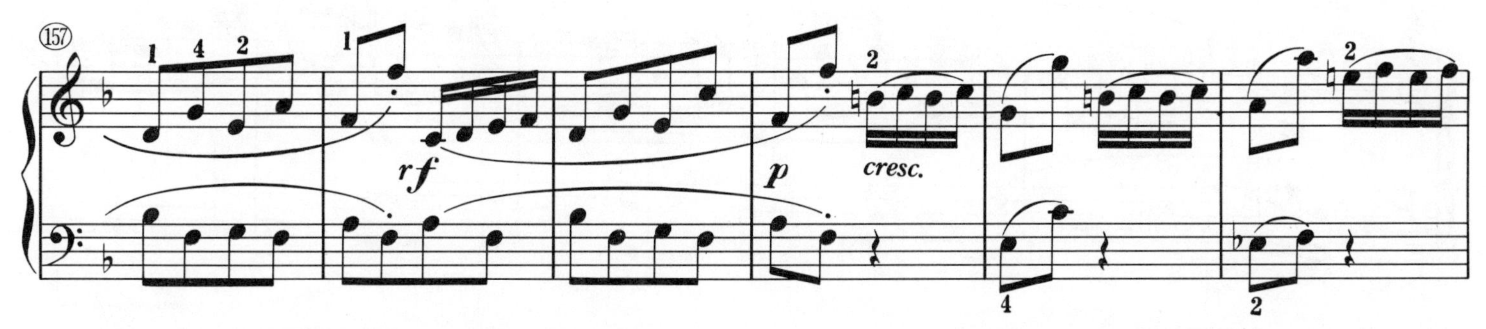
rf
p
cresc.

f
sf
p

cresc.
dim.
p

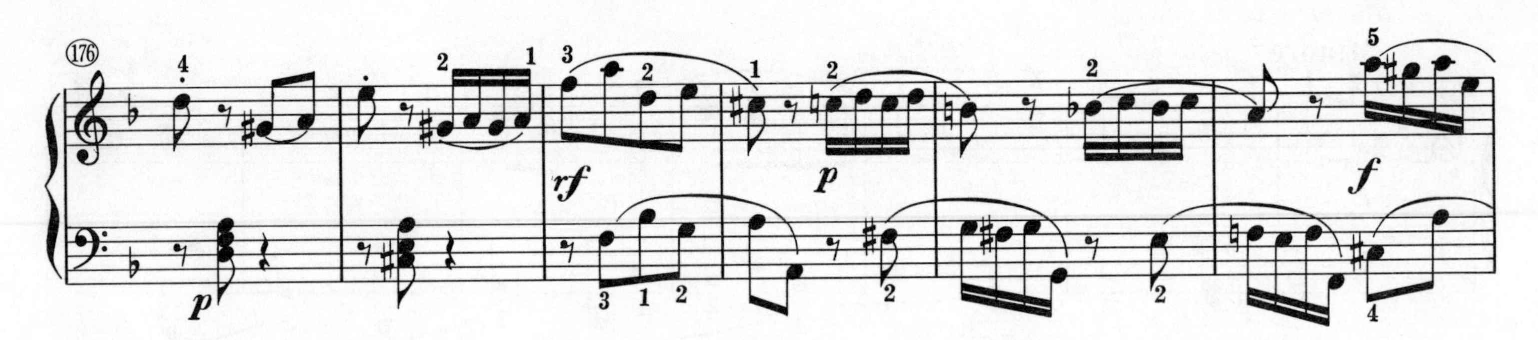
rf
p
f

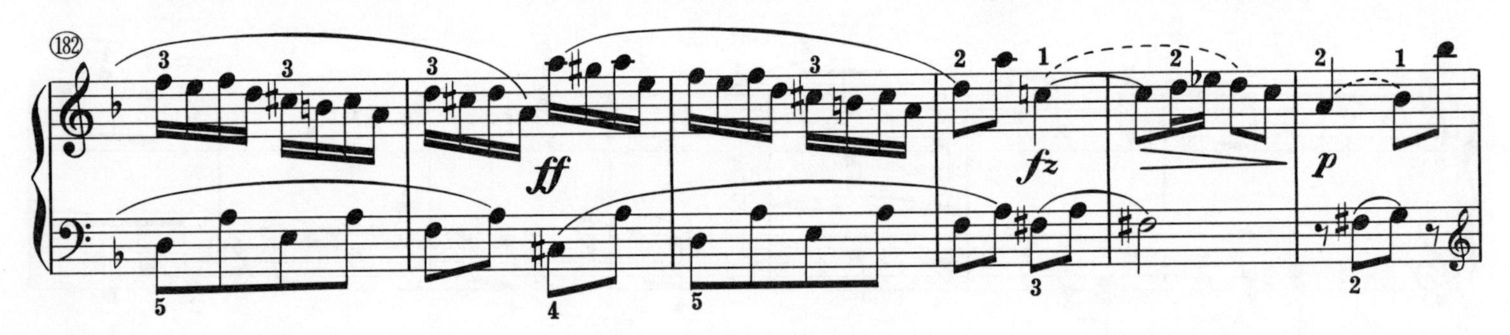
ff
fz
p

mf
f

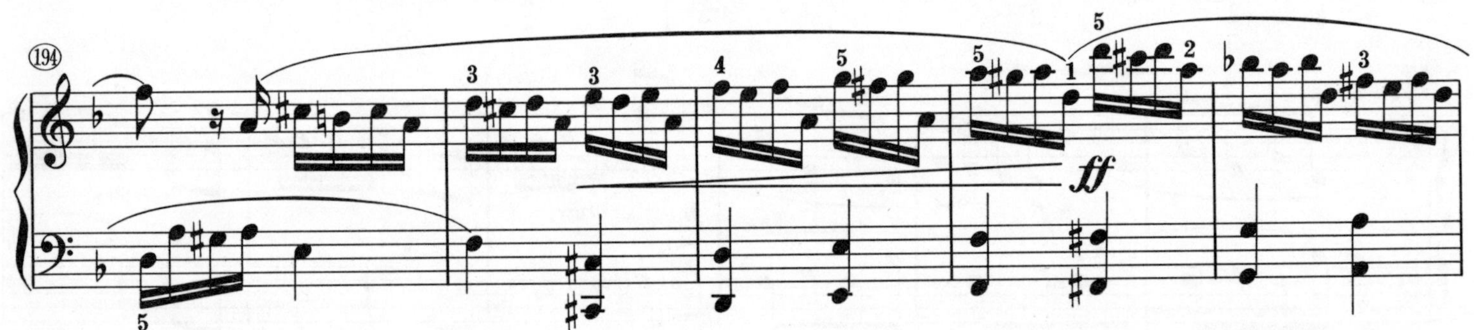
ff

sf
p
poco
cresc.
mf
dim.

rit.
p
calando
pp

Maggiore

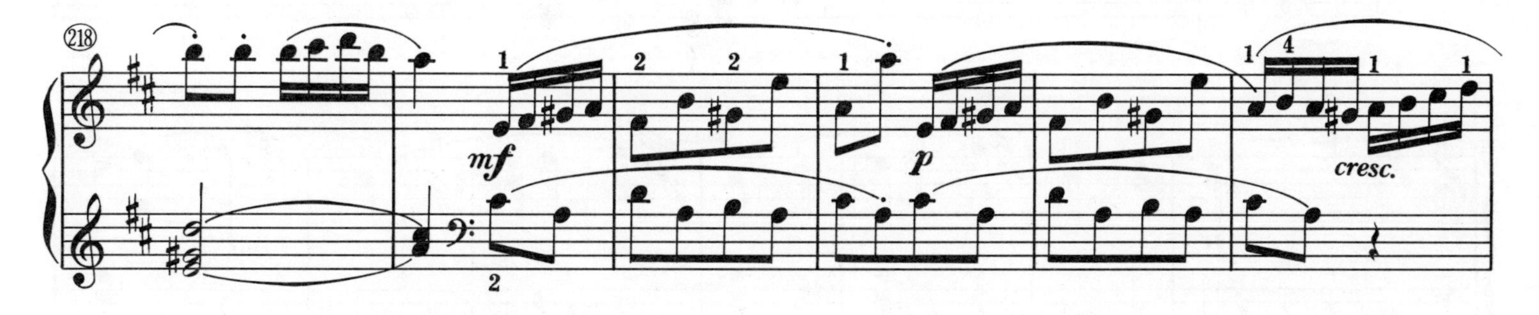

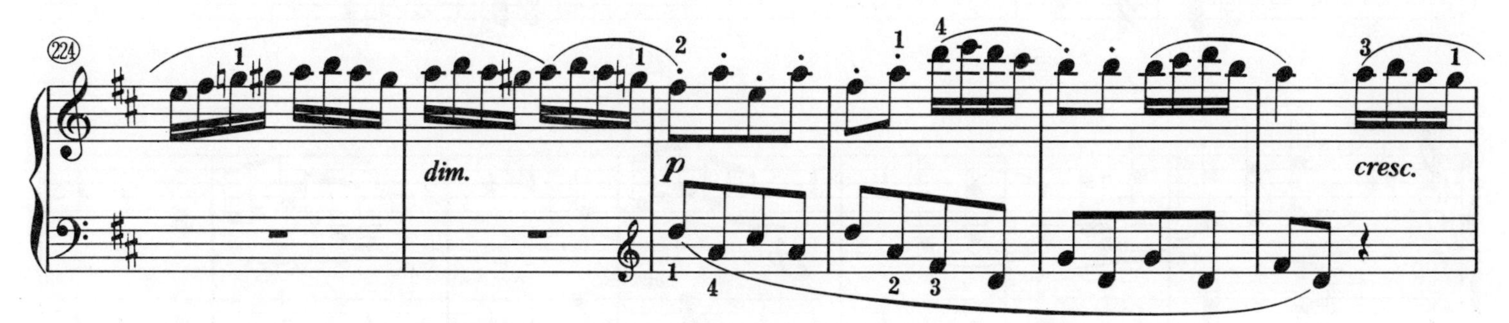

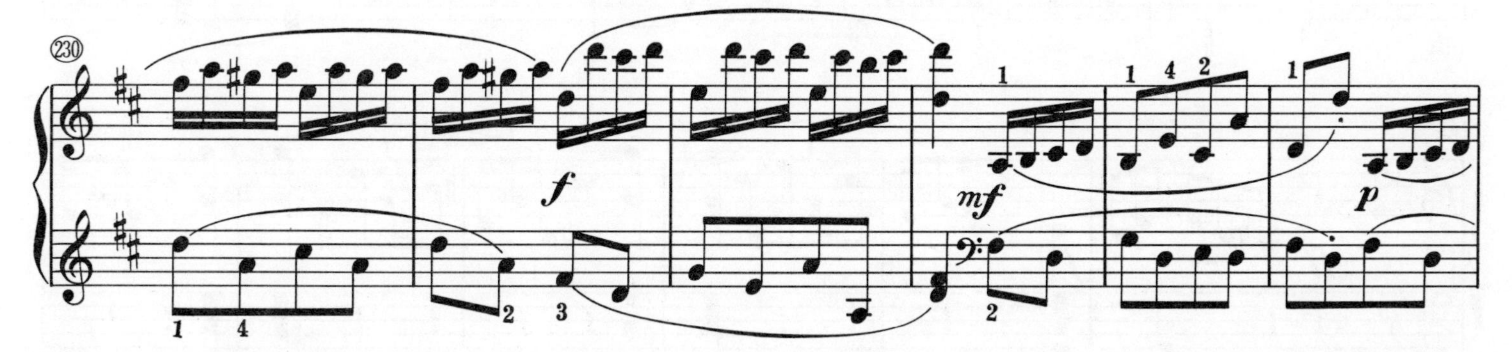

SONATA

Op. 10, No. 1

Allegro molto e con brio

Ludwig van Beethoven

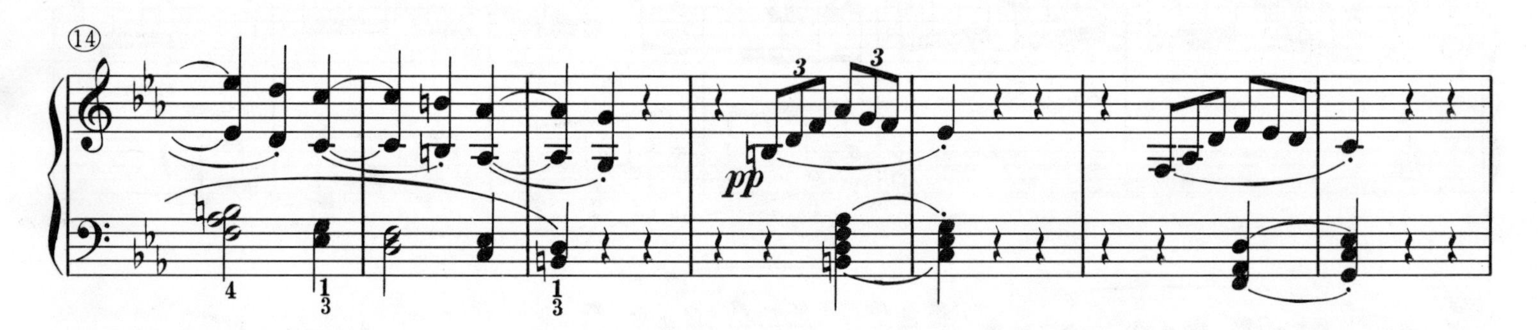

48
p

56

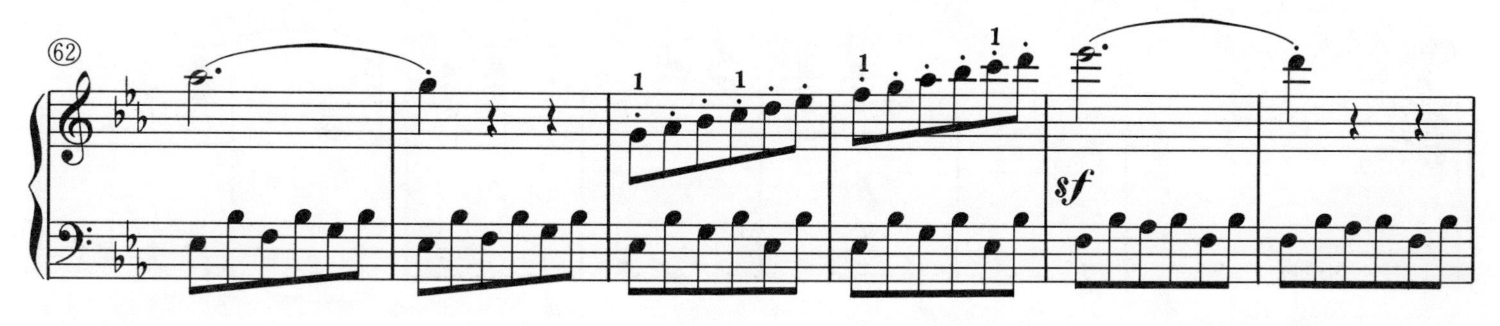
62
sf

68
cresc.
sf
sf

74
f
tr
f
sf

80
sf
sf
cresc.
ff

86
sf
sf
sf
ff

92
ff
sf
fp
p
fp

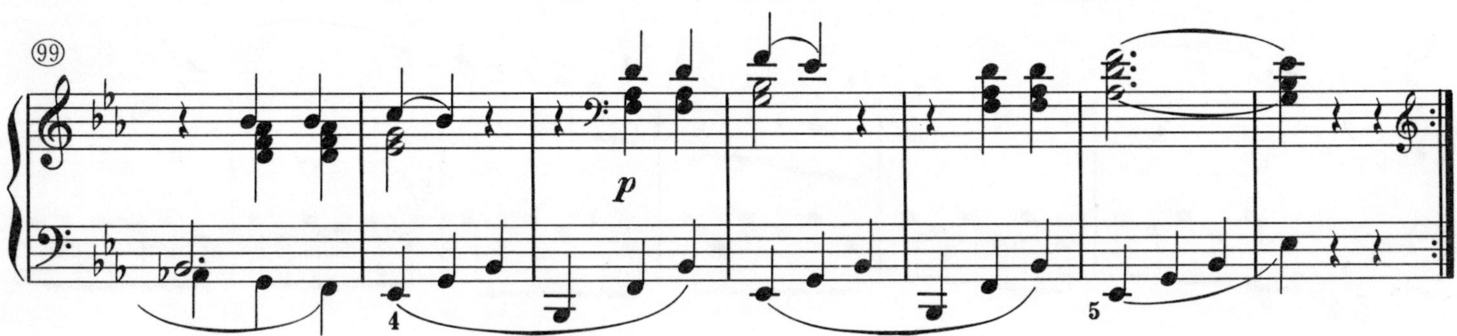
99
p

106
f
p
f
p

113
f
p

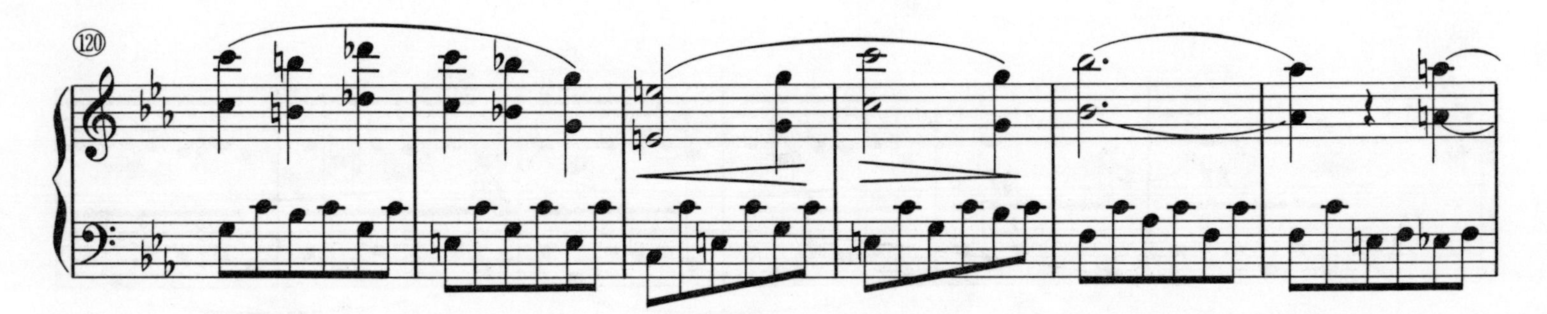
120

126

132

138
cresc.
sf

146
cresc.
sf
f
sf

154
ff
sf
sf
p
p

162
decresc.
f

169
p
f
p

175
rinf.

182
pp

188
ff
ff
fp

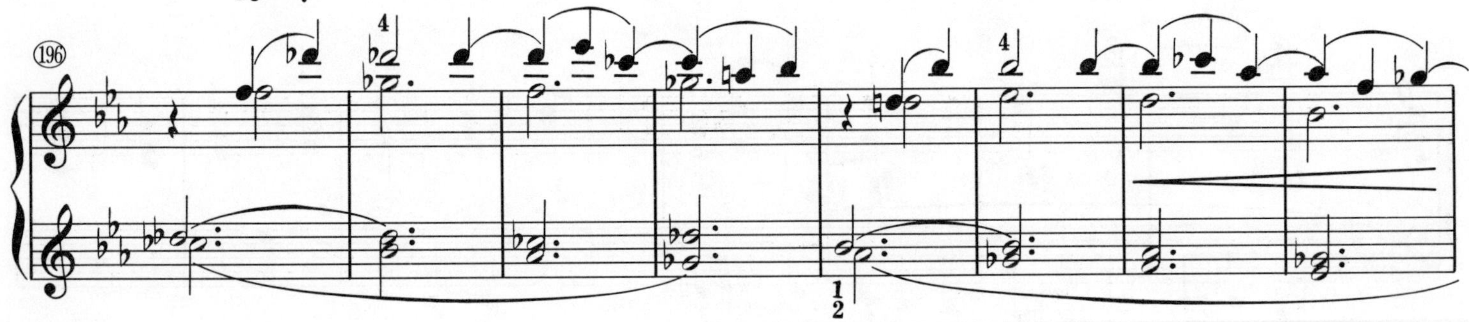
196

204
p

212

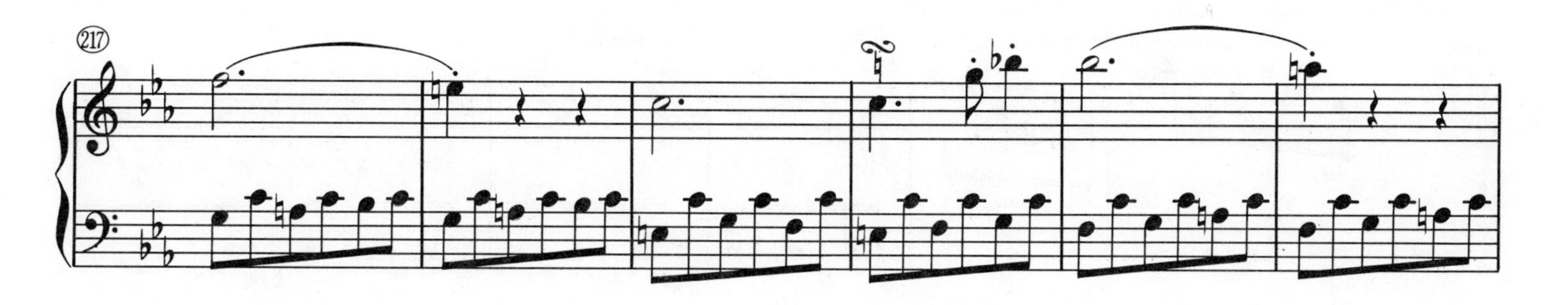
217

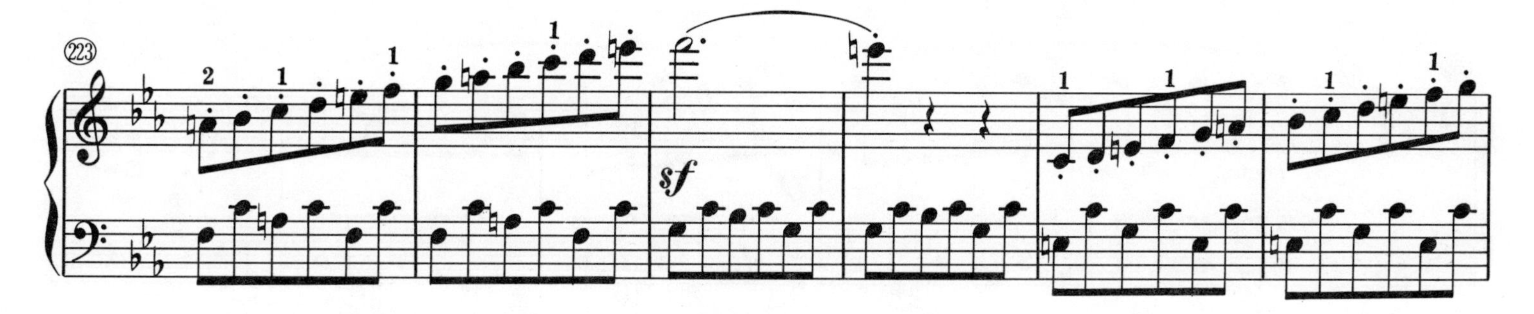
223
sf

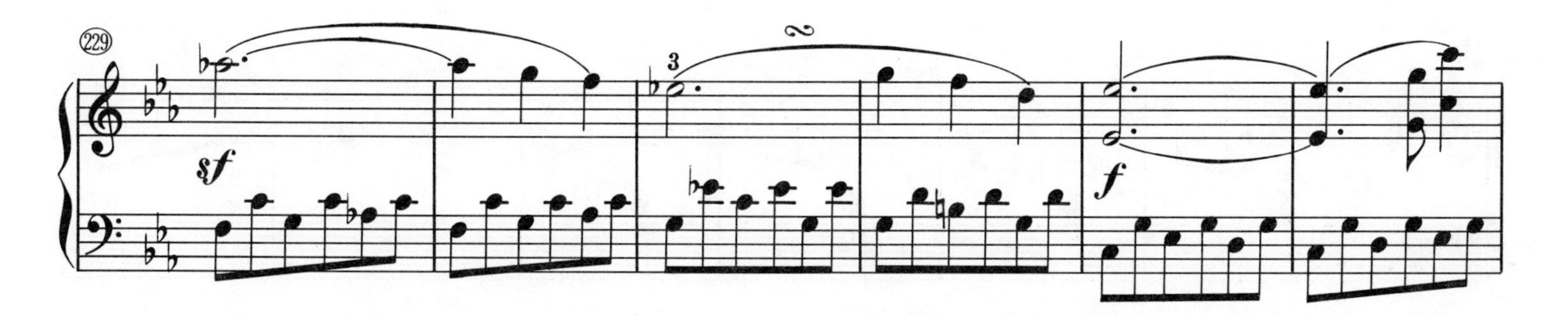
229
sf
f

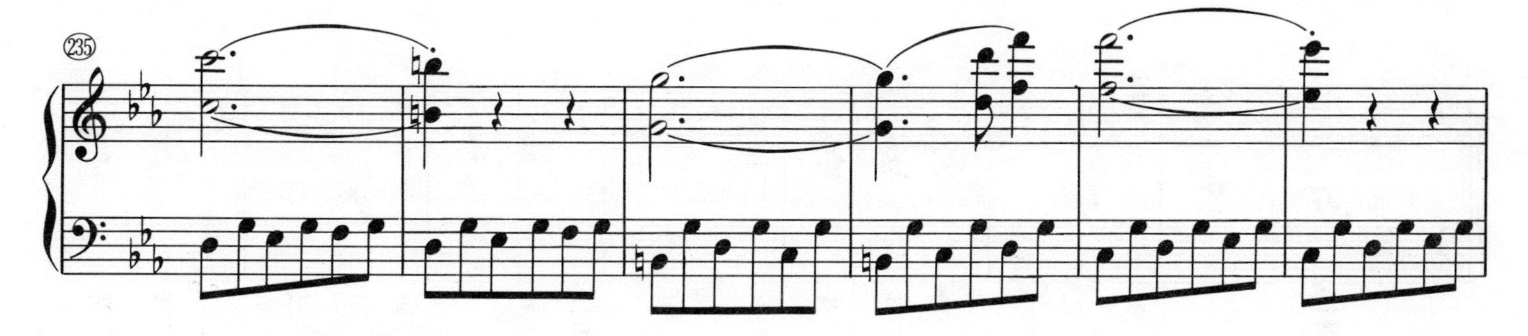
235

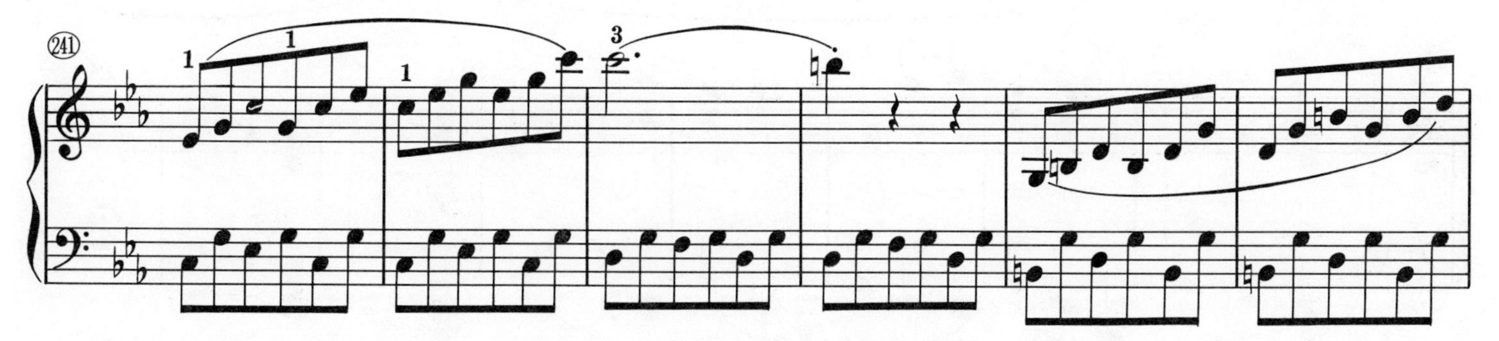
241

247
cresc.
sf
sf
sf
sf
tr

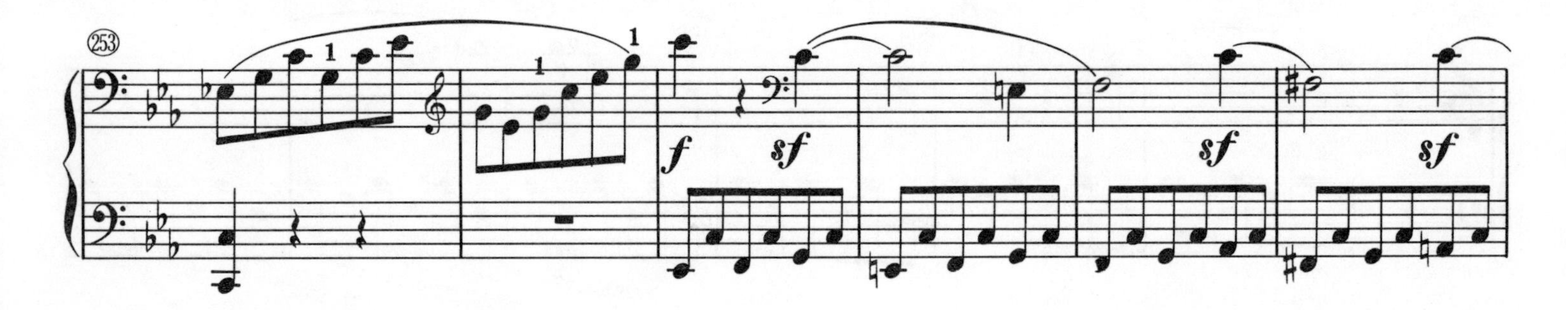
253
f
sf
sf
sf

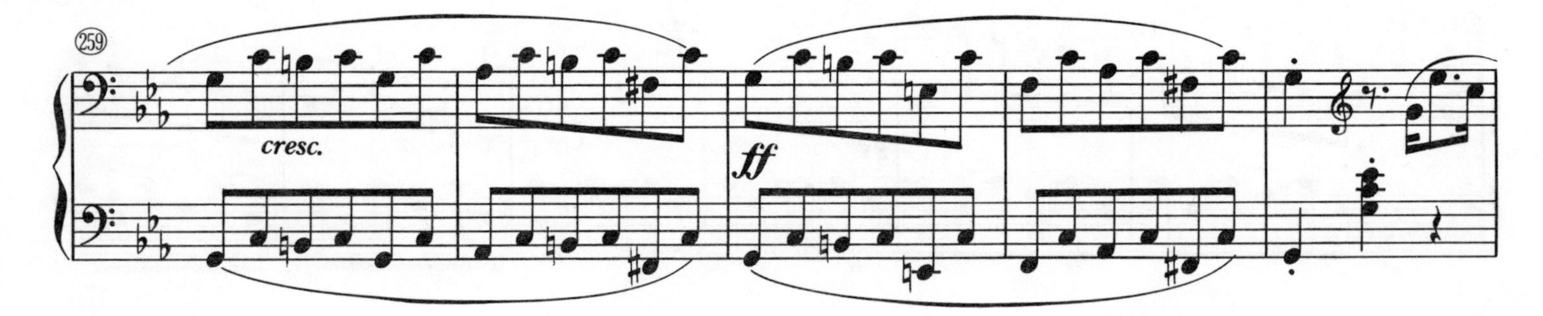
259
cresc.
ff

264
sf
sf
sf
ff

270
ff
sf
fp
p
fp

277
p
ff

Adagio molto

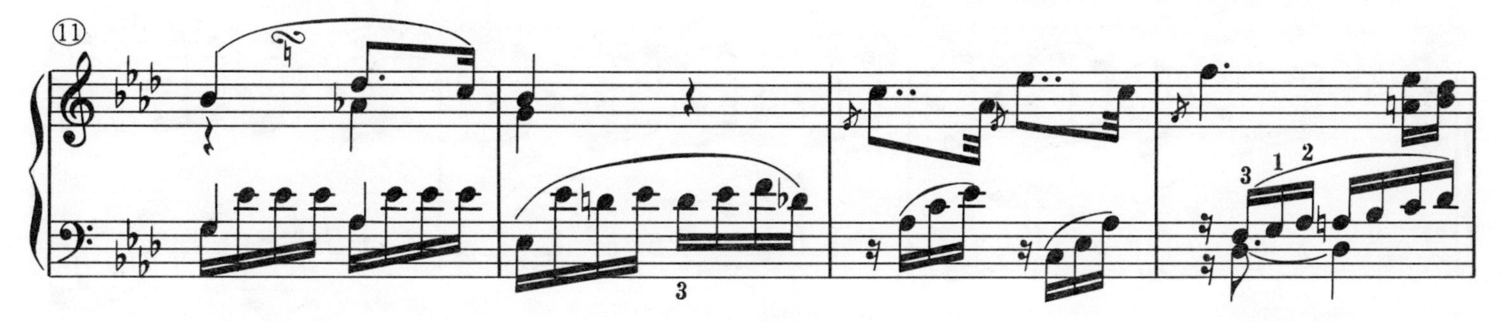

29
cresc.

32
sf
p

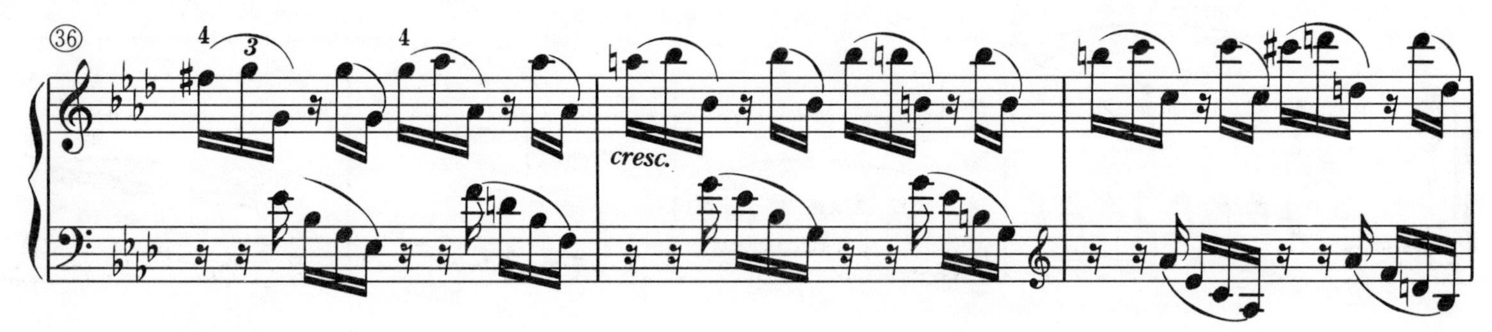
36
cresc.

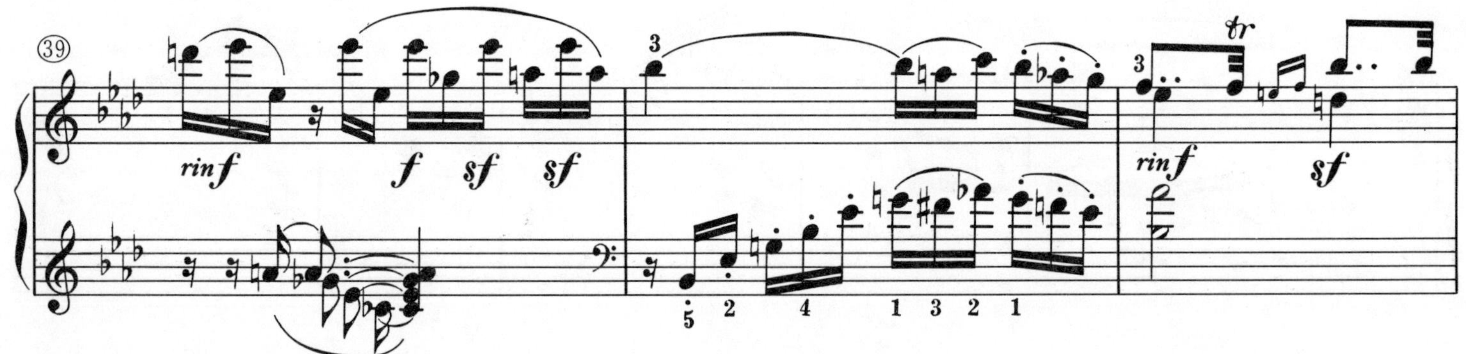
39
rinf
f
sf
sf
rinf
sf

42
f
rinf
sfp
ff

46
p
cresc.

51
sf
sf
tr

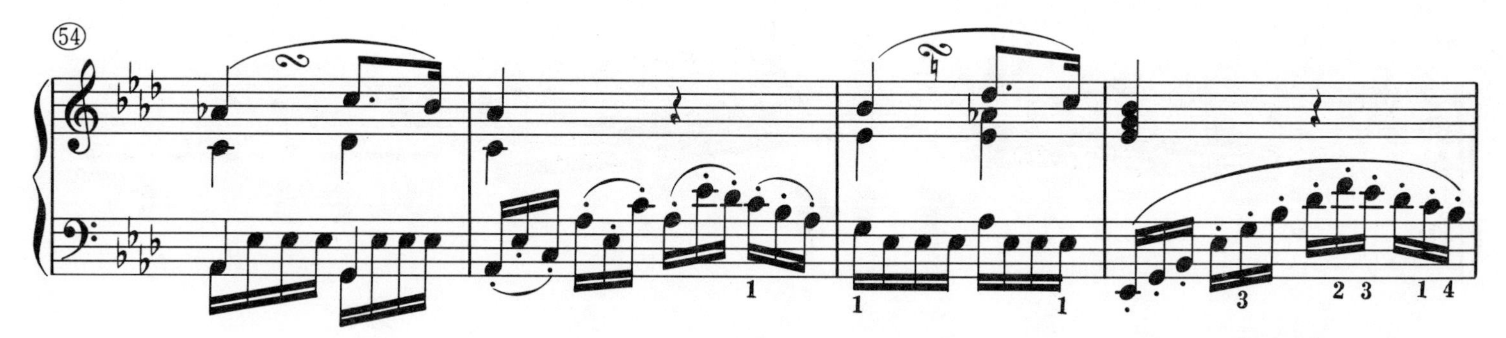
54

58

61
ff
p
ff
p

65
ff
fp
fp
fp

70
pp

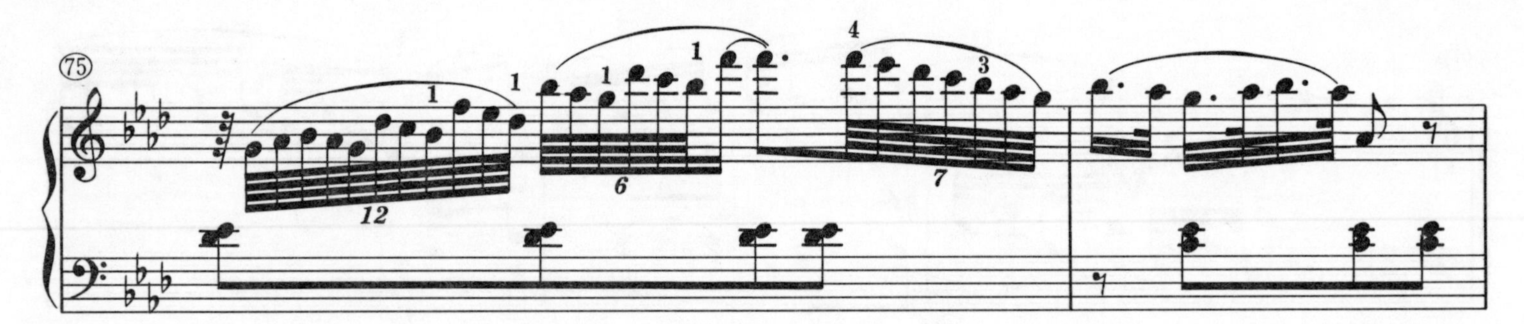
75
12
6
7

77
12
11
cresc.

79
sf
p

83
pp
cresc.

86
rinf
f
sf
sf
p
tr
rinf
sf

89
f
tr
rinf.
sf
p

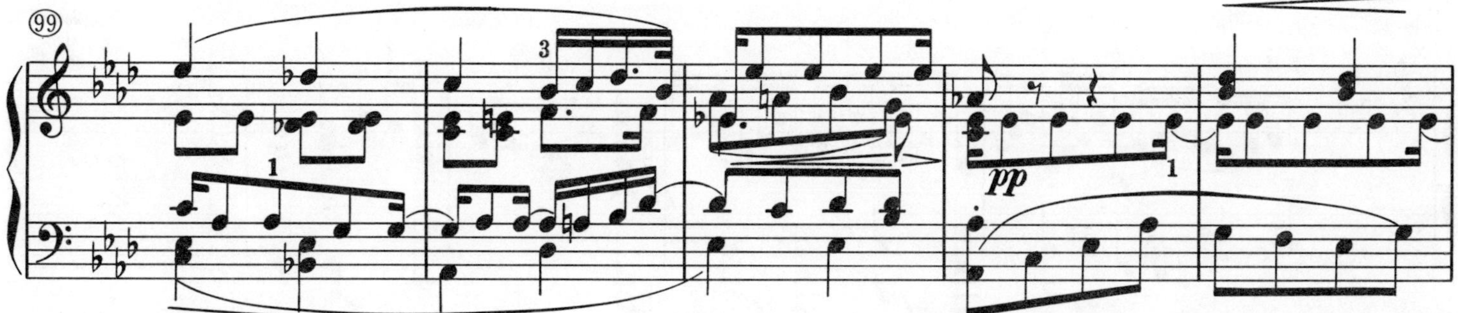

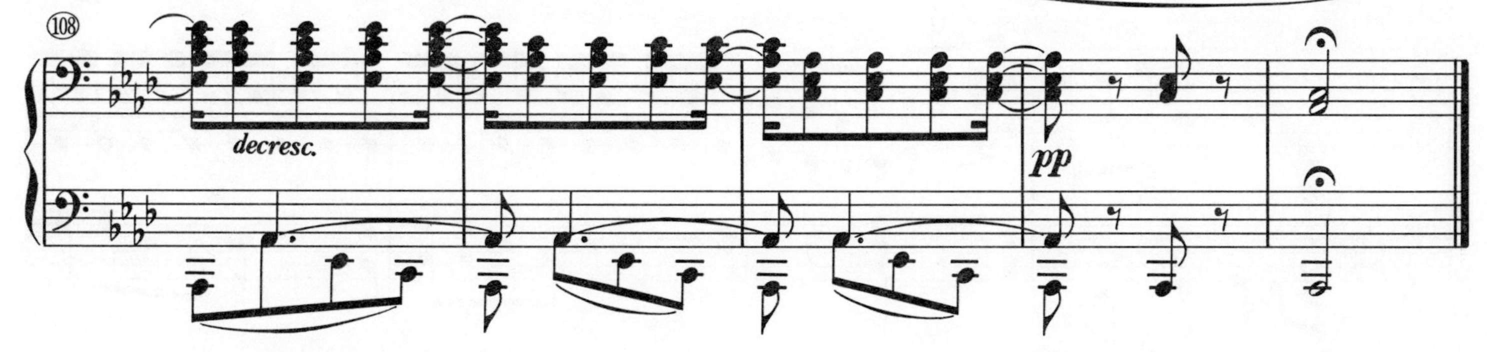

Finale
Prestissimo

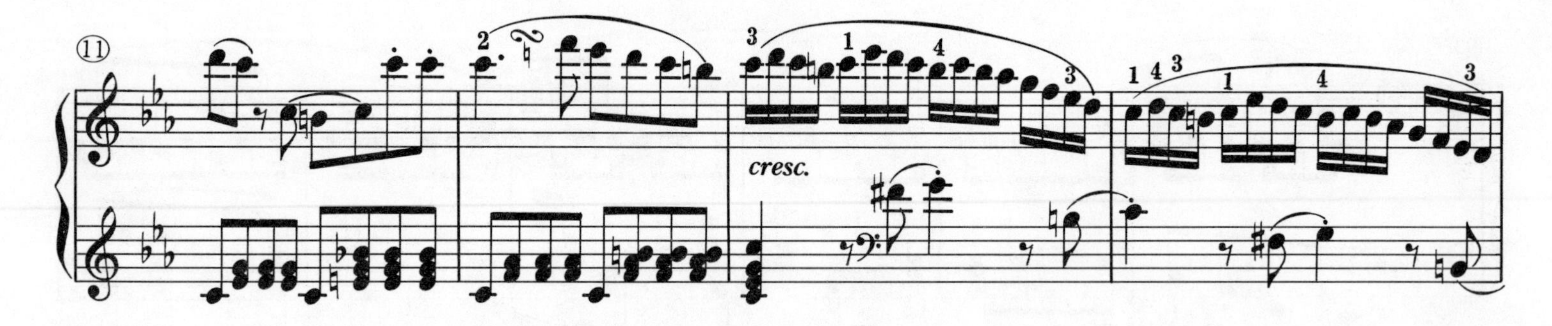
11
cresc.

15
f
sf
ff
p

20
ff(p)
fp

27

31
ff

34
ff

cresc.

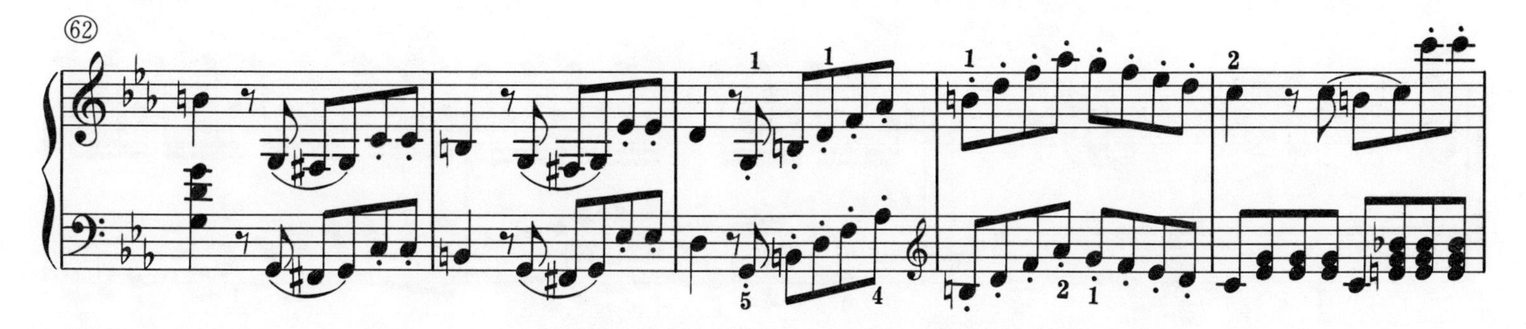

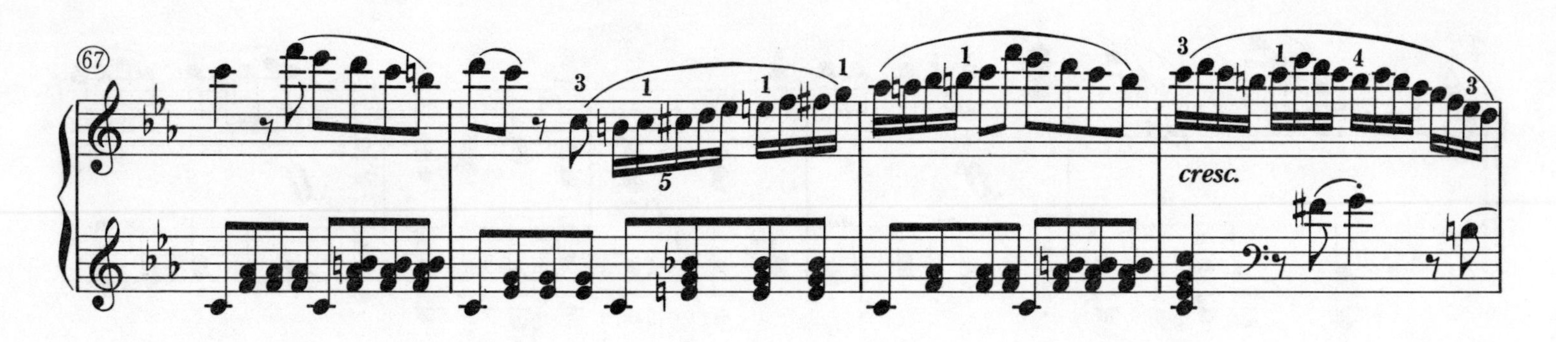
67
cresc.

71
f
sf
sf
sf
ff
p

ffp

81
fp
fp

86
cresc.
sf
ff

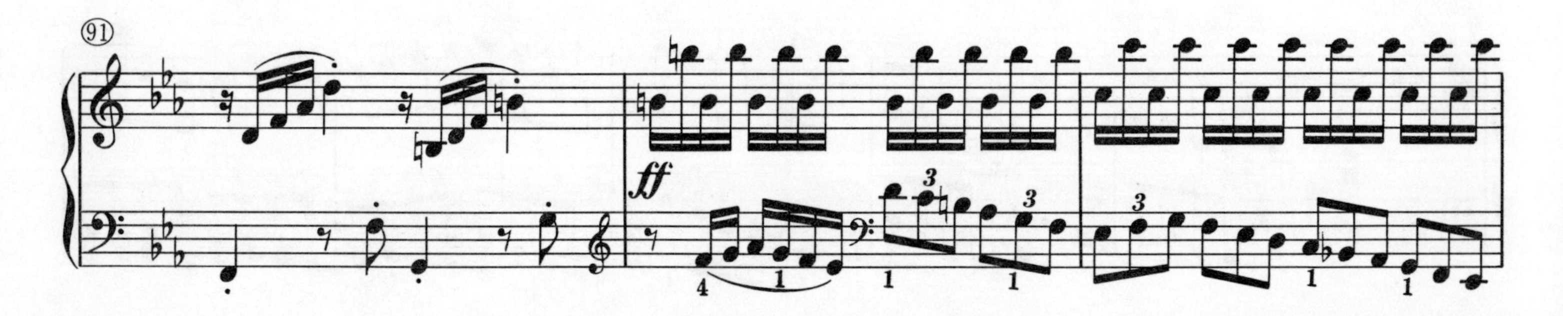
91
ff

94
ff
p

98
ff
ff
p

103
cresc.
fp
pp
p ritard.
calando
Adagio
109
tenuto
tenuto

115
Tempo I
ff
p

119
decresc.
(p)

SONATA

Op. 120

Allegro moderato

Franz Schubert

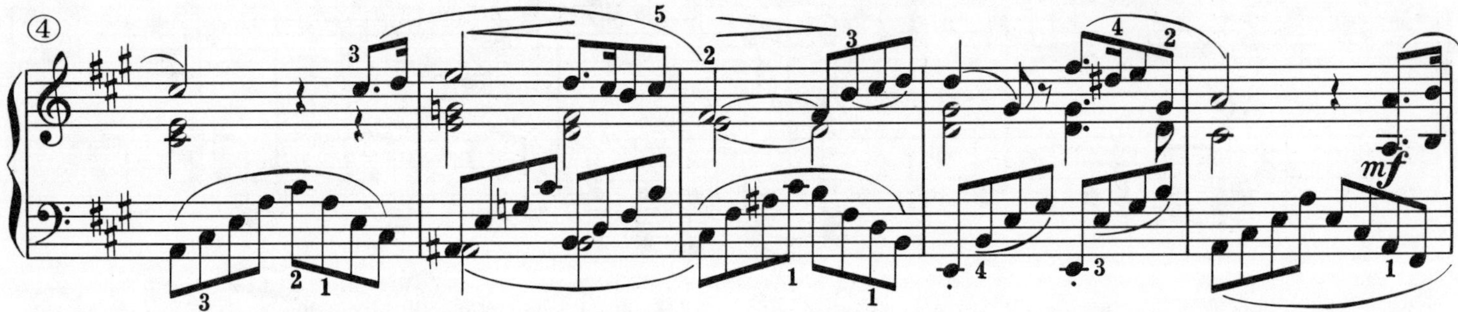

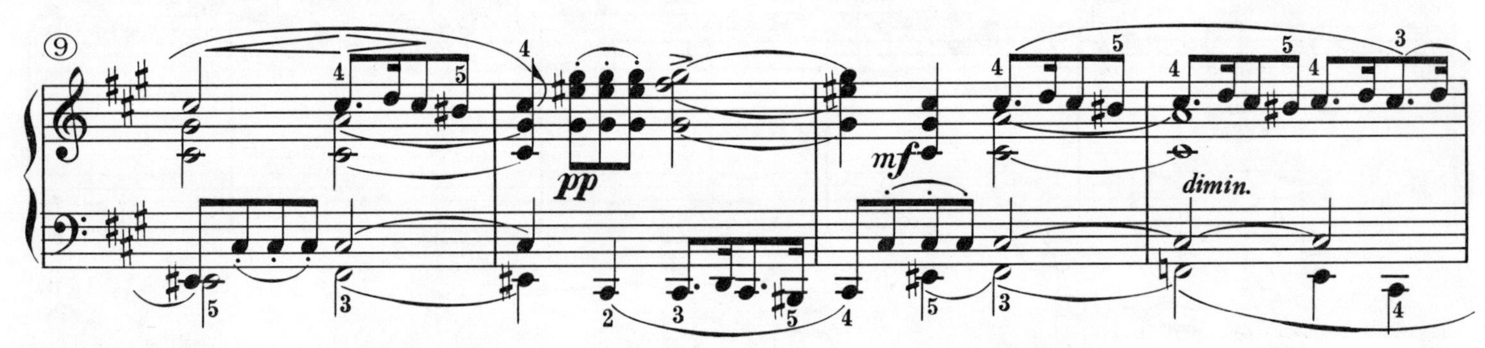

25

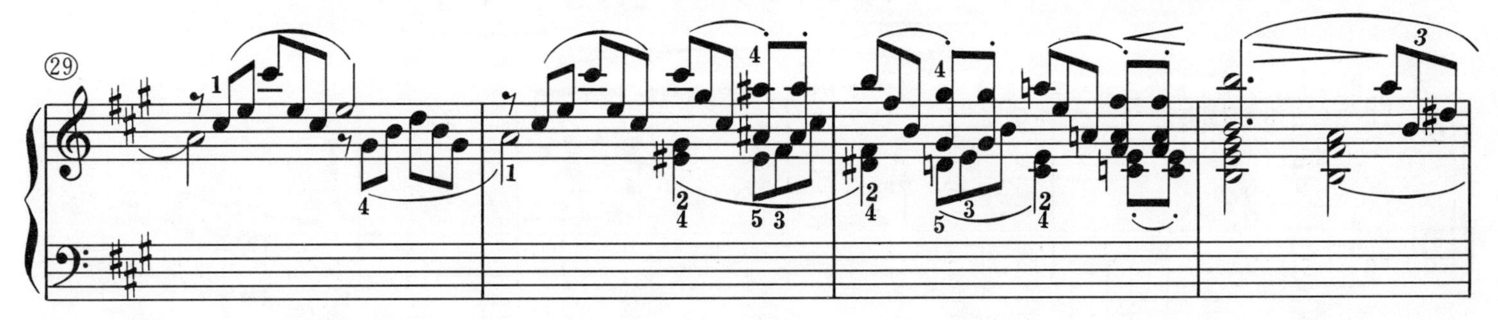
29

33
cresc.
mf
f

37
decresc.

40
p
pp

44
ppp

p
mf

53
pp
mf
decresc.
fz
fz
f
58
fz

61
fz
fz

64
8
fz
p

68
pp

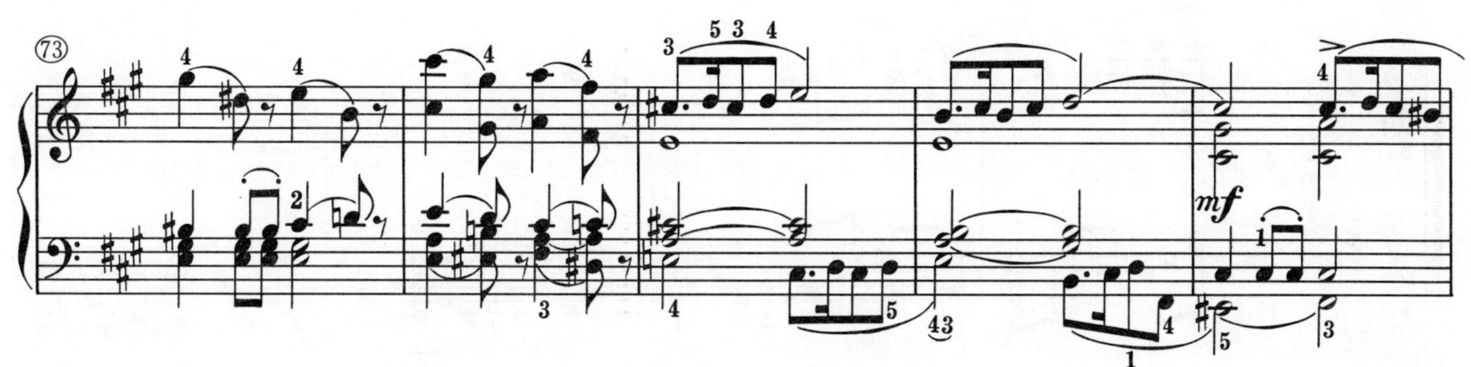
73
mf

78
decresc.
p

83

88
mf
pp
mf
decresc.

92
p

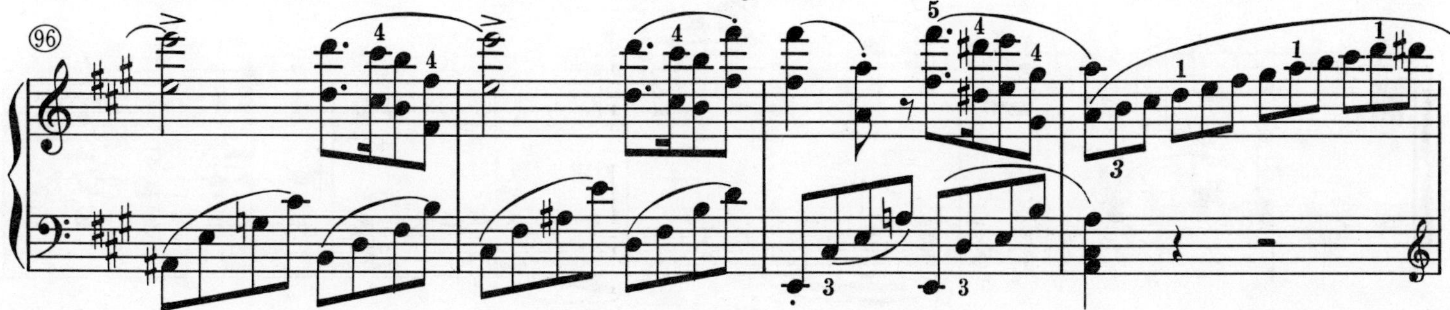
96

100
legato

104

108

112
cresc.
mf
f

116
decresc.

119
p
pp

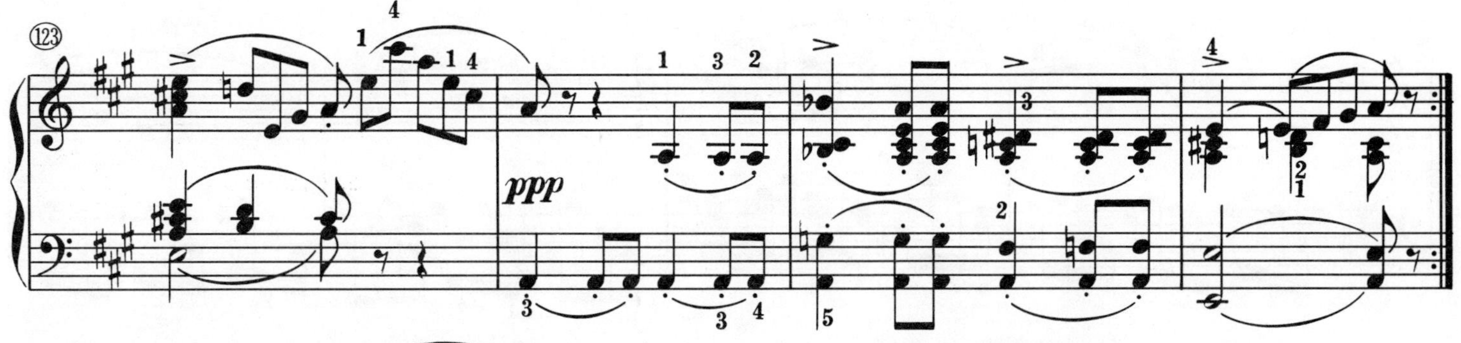
123
ppp

127
pp
pp

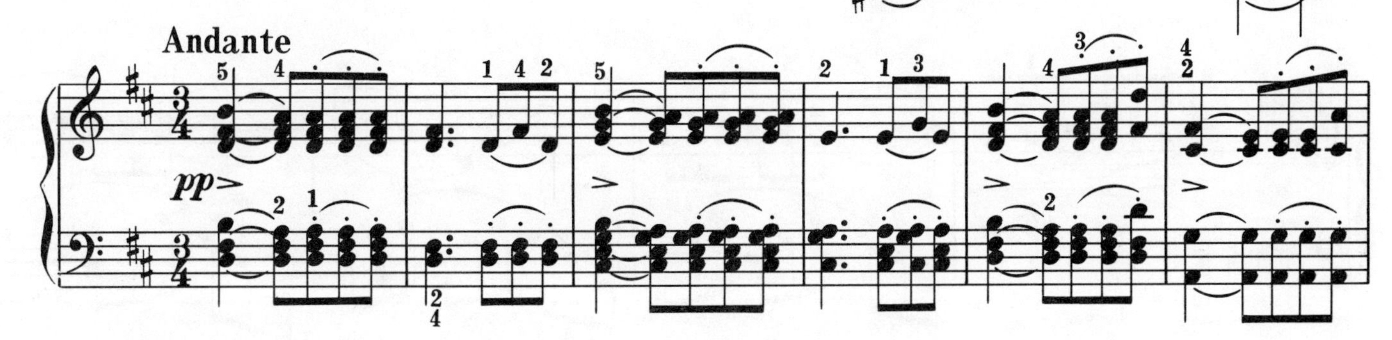
Andante
pp

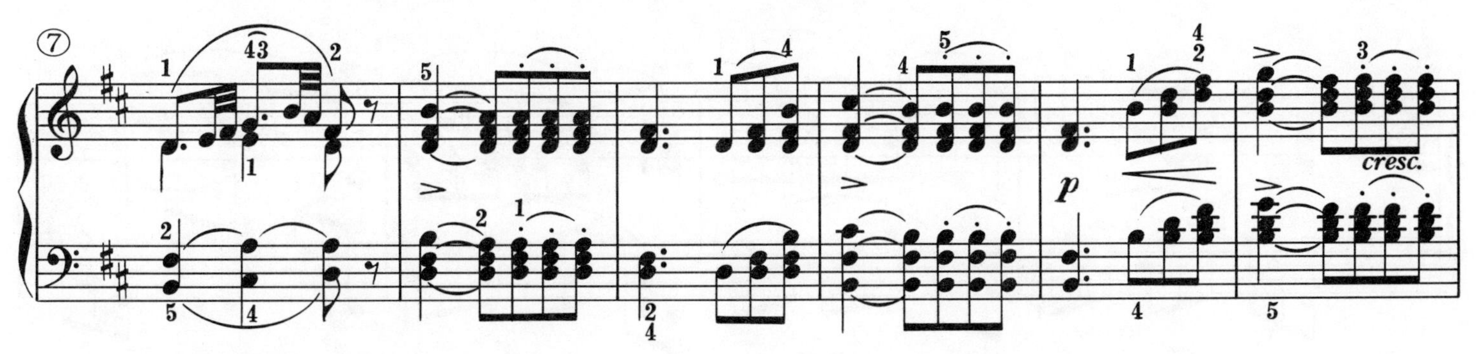
7
p
cresc.

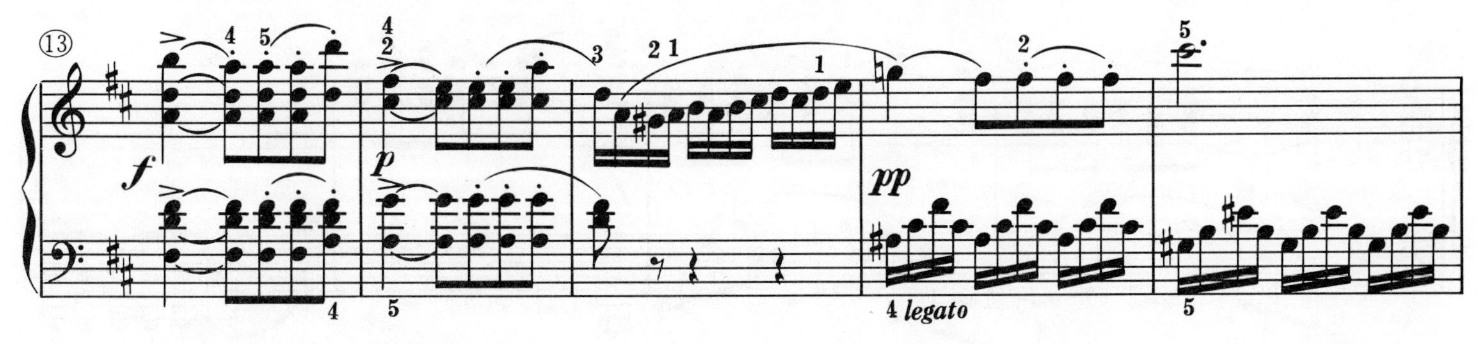
13
f
p
pp
legato

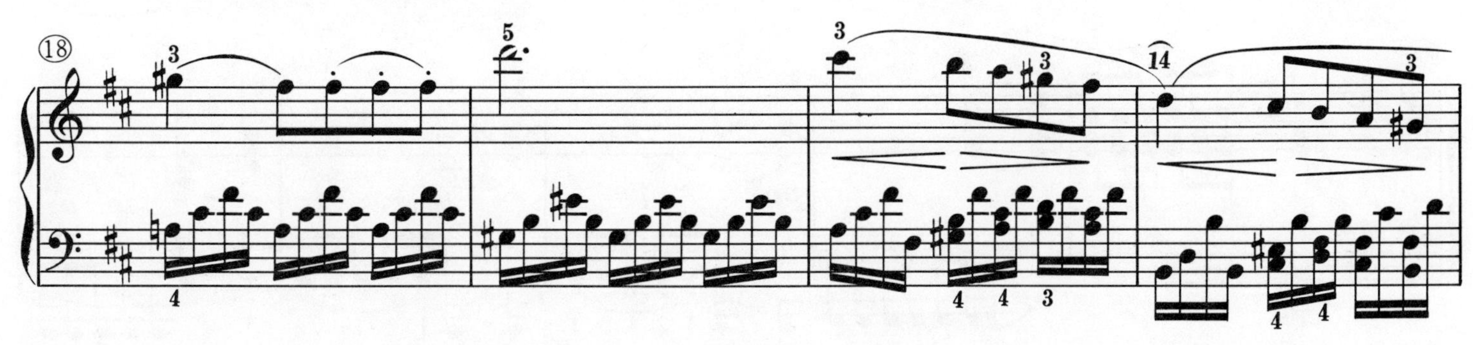
18

22

26
pp
cresc.

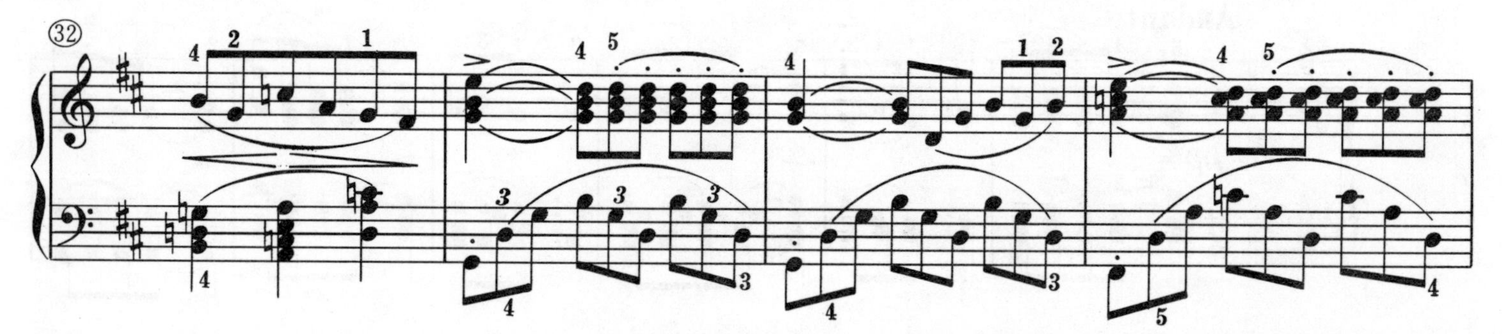
32

36

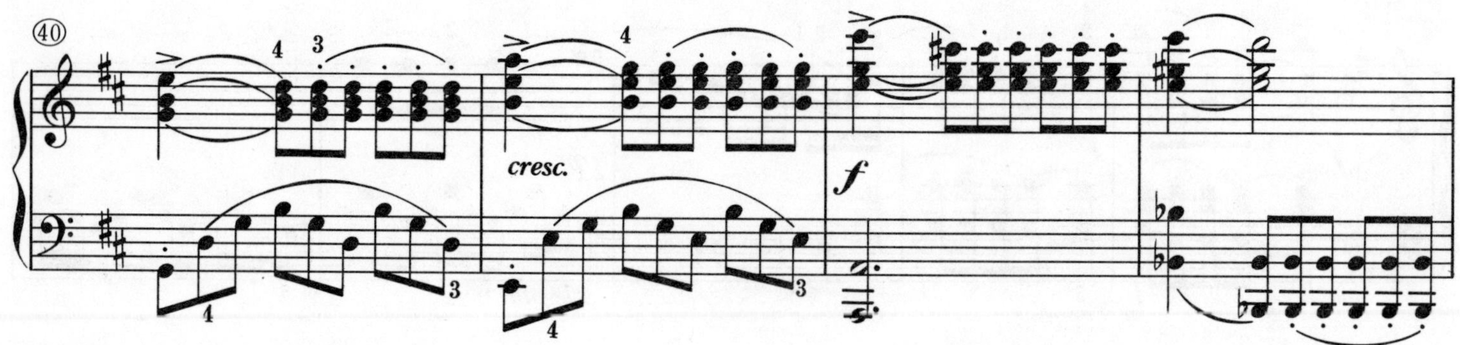
40
cresc.
f

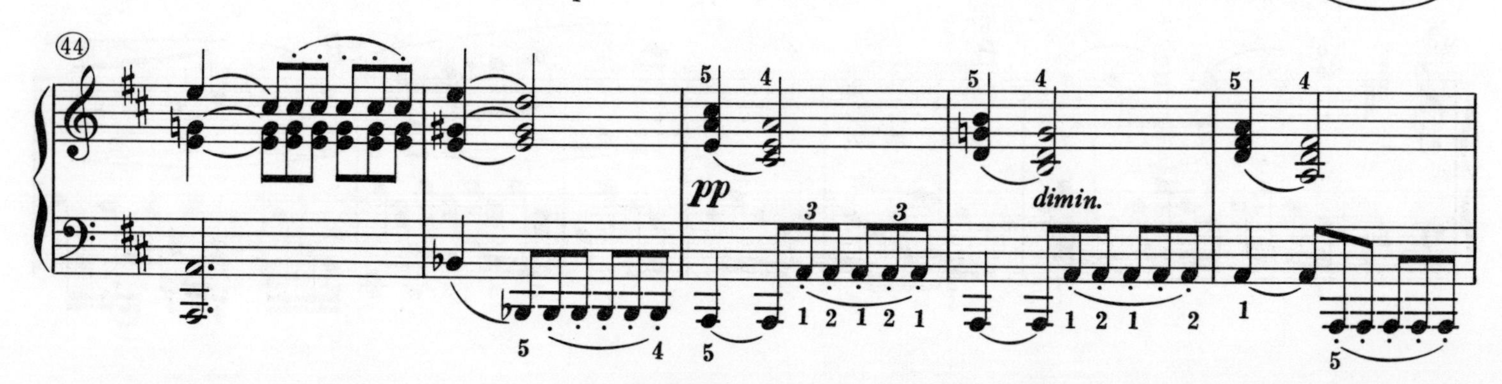
44
pp
dimin.

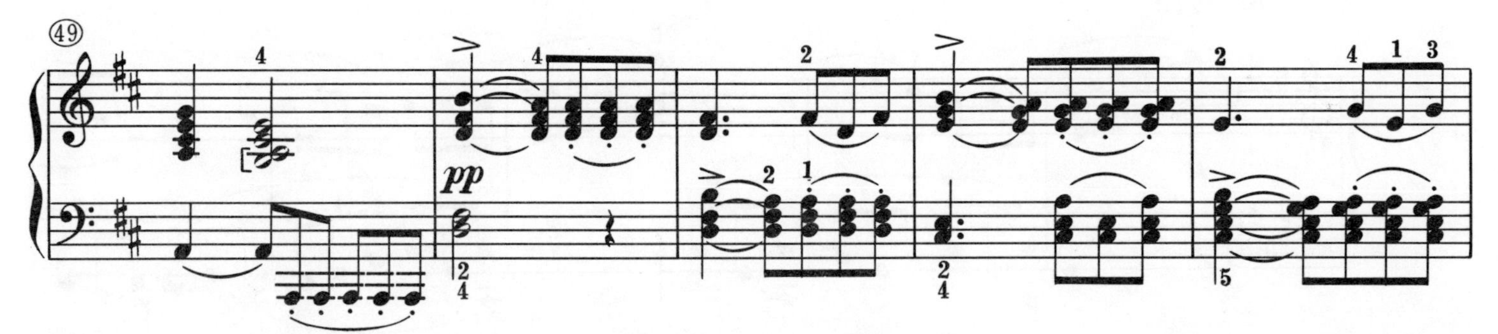
49
pp

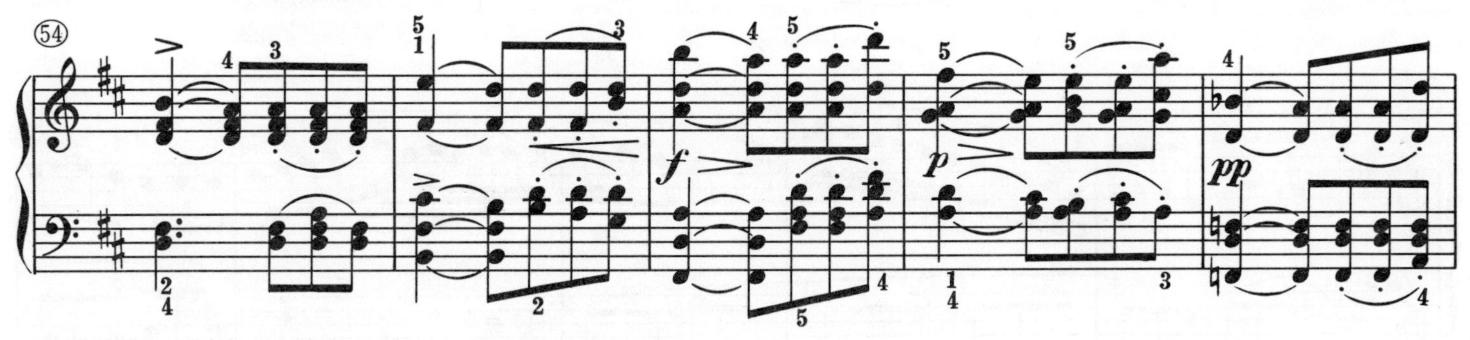
54
f
p
pp

59
legato

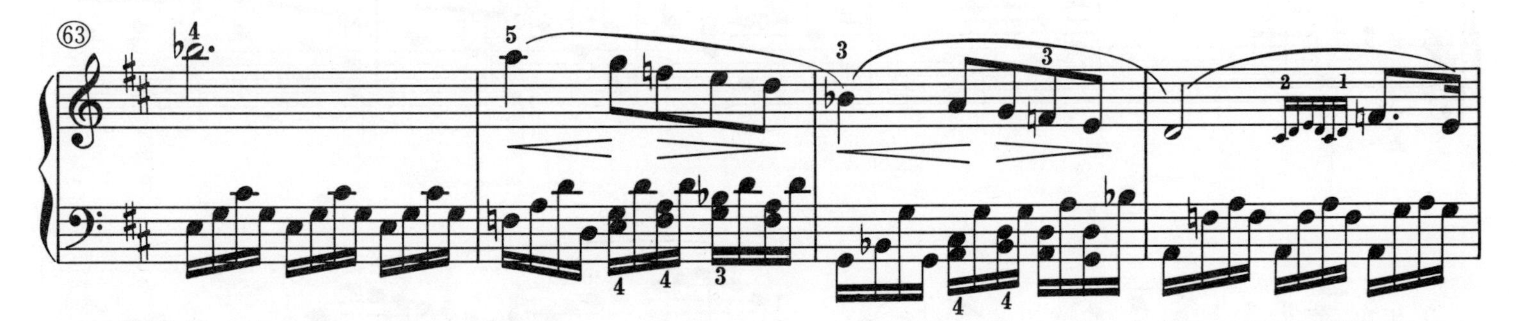
63

67

70
pp

Allegro

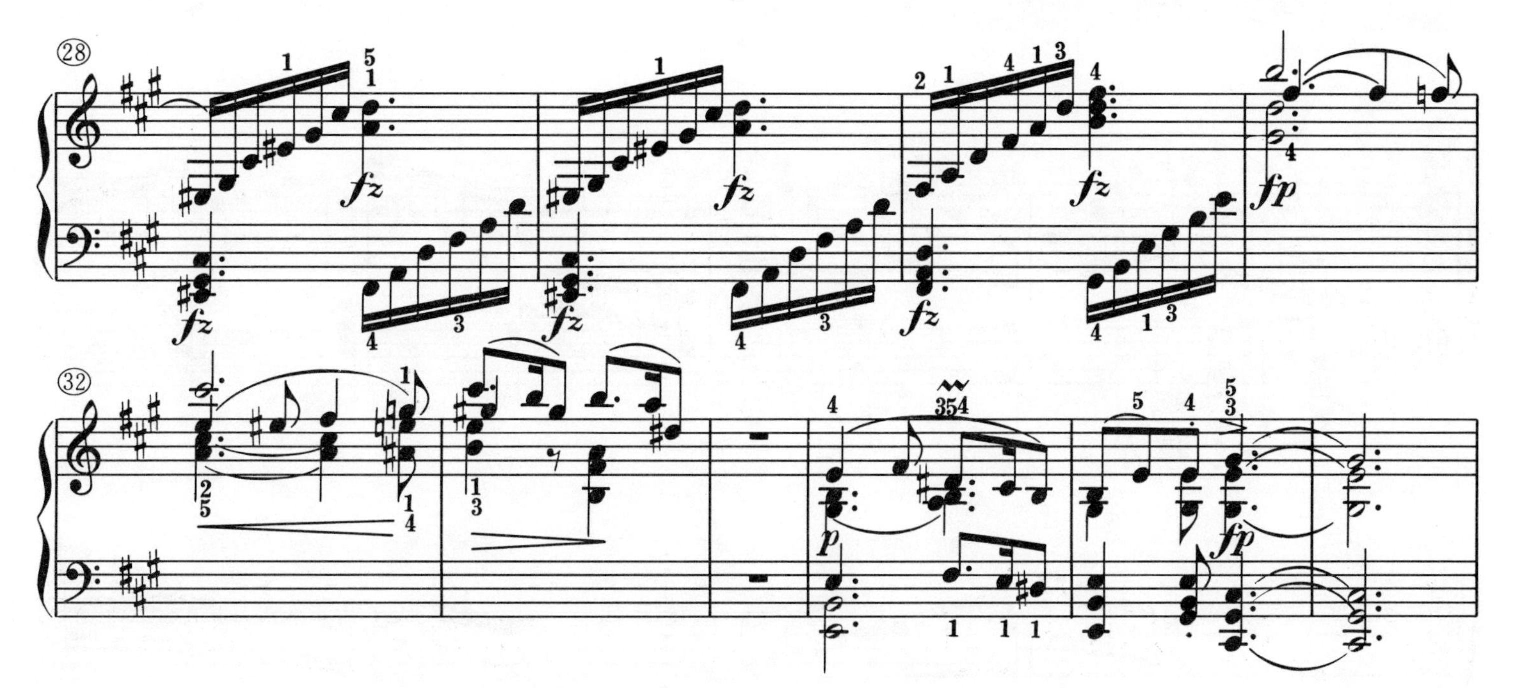

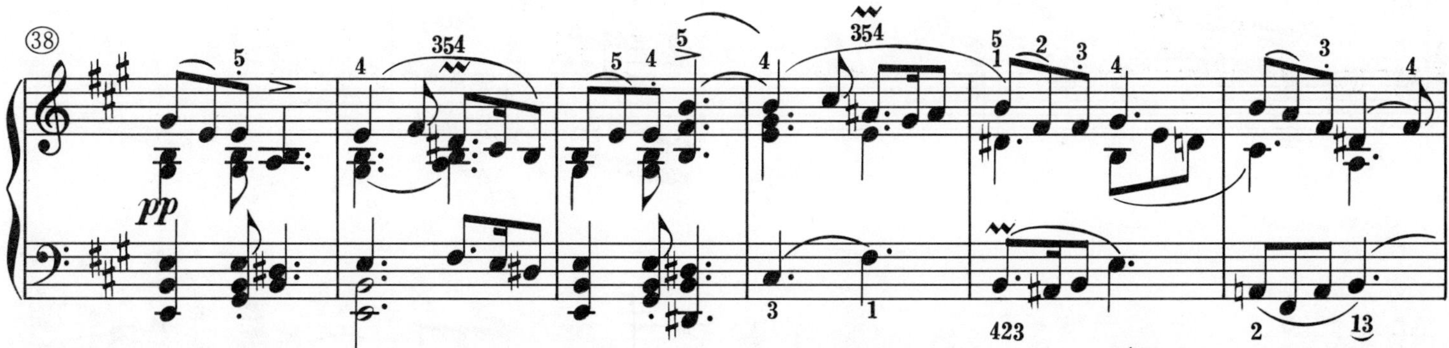

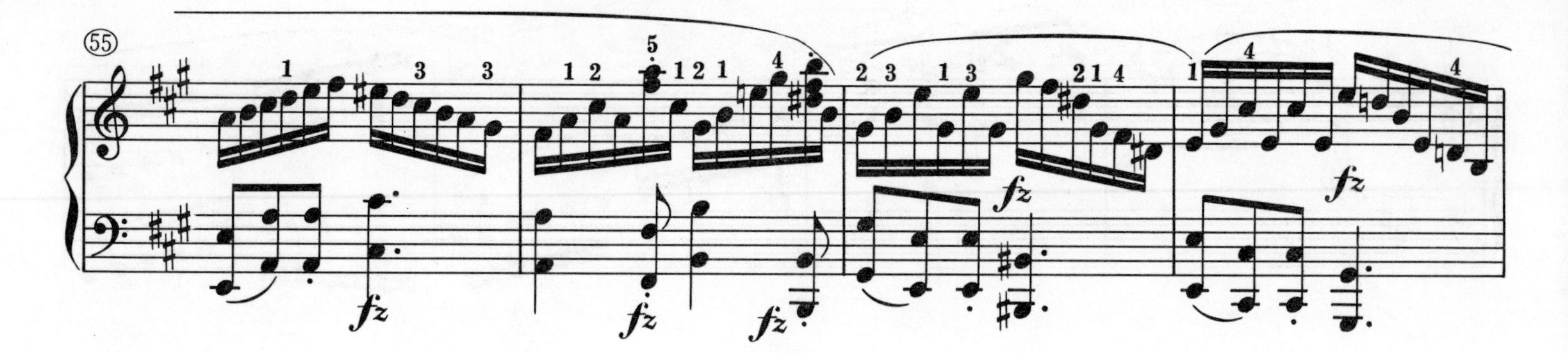
55
fz
fz
fz
fz
fz

59
fz
fz
fz
p legato

63
8
ff

67
8
fz
fz
fz
fz
p

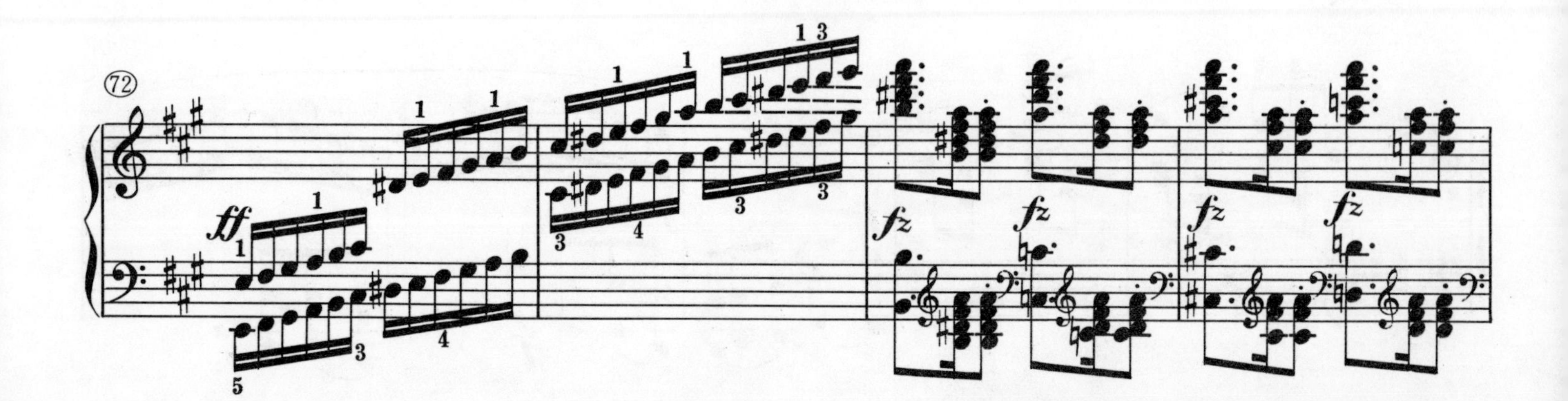
72
ff
fz
fz
fz
fz

76
p
ff

80
8
p

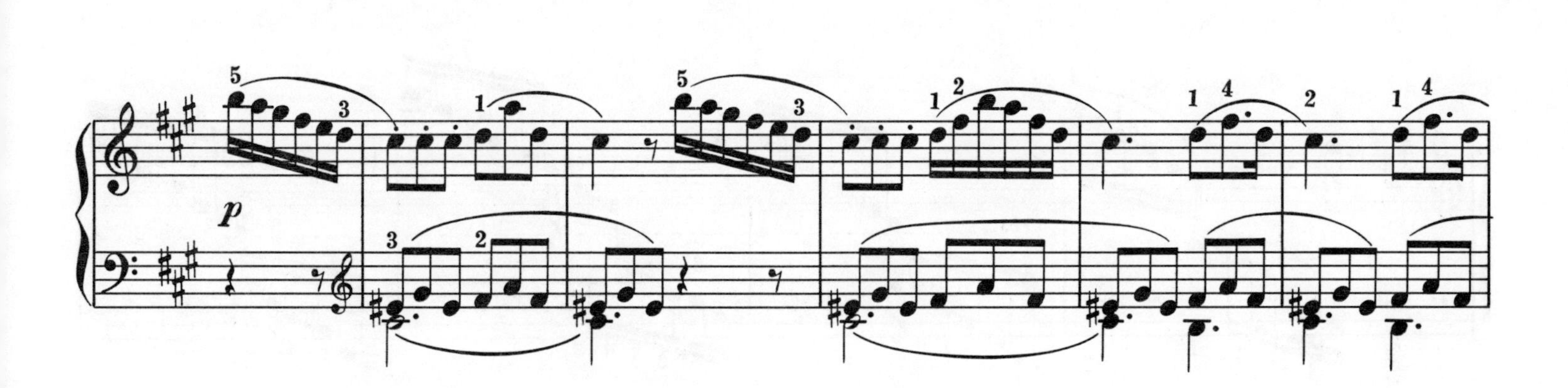
p

90
pp

95
f

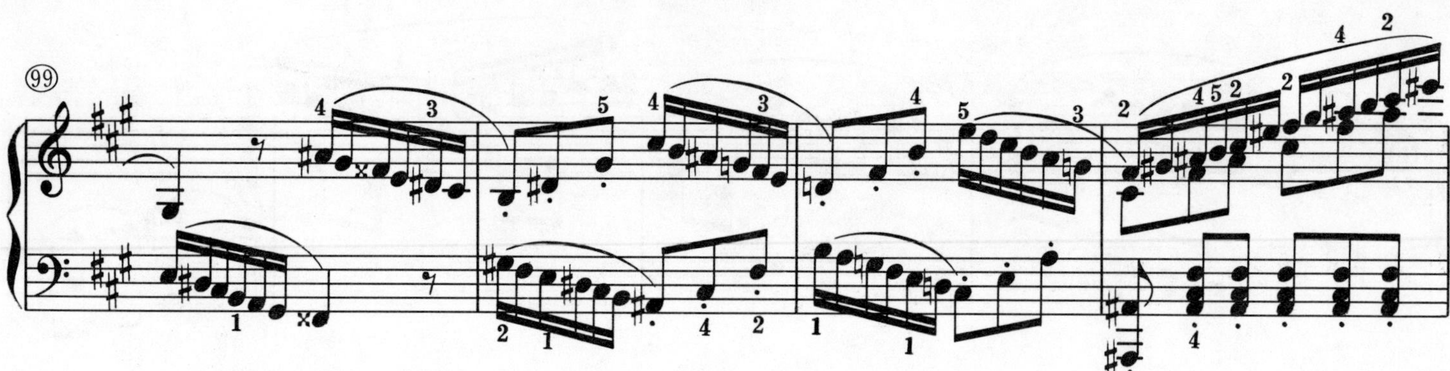

cresc.
decresc.
p

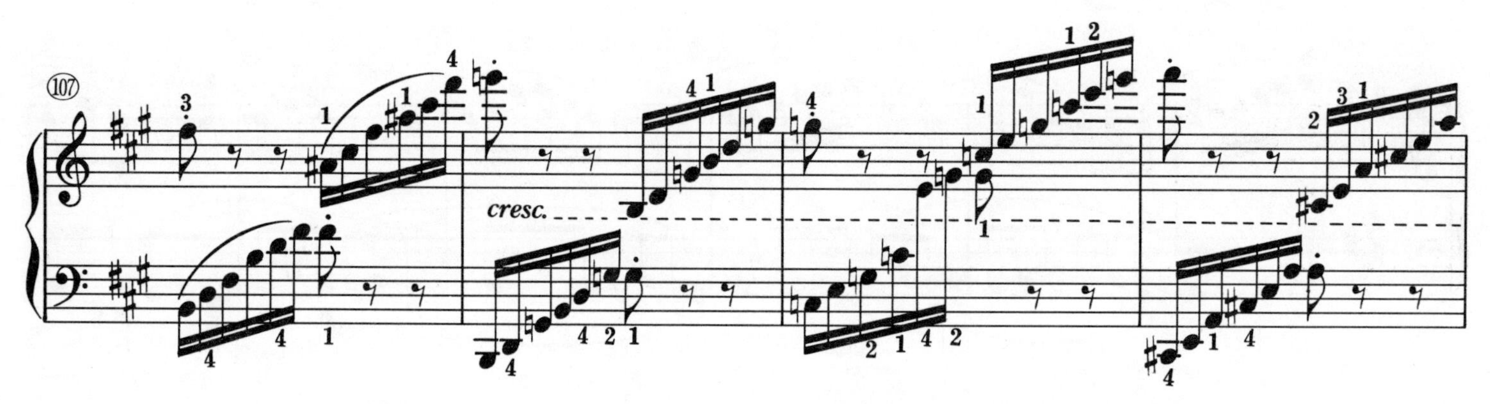
cresc.

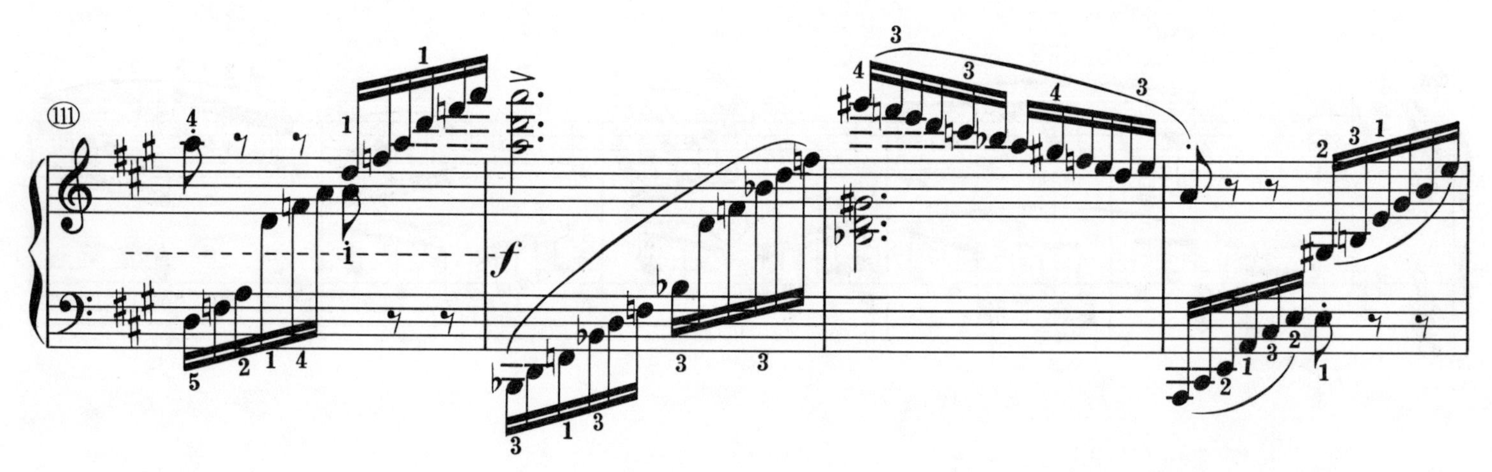
f

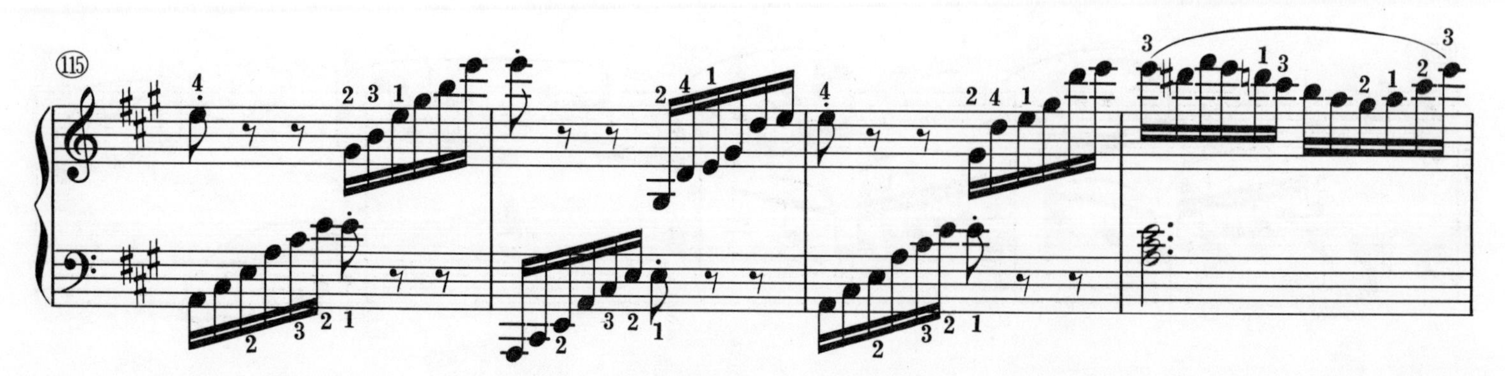

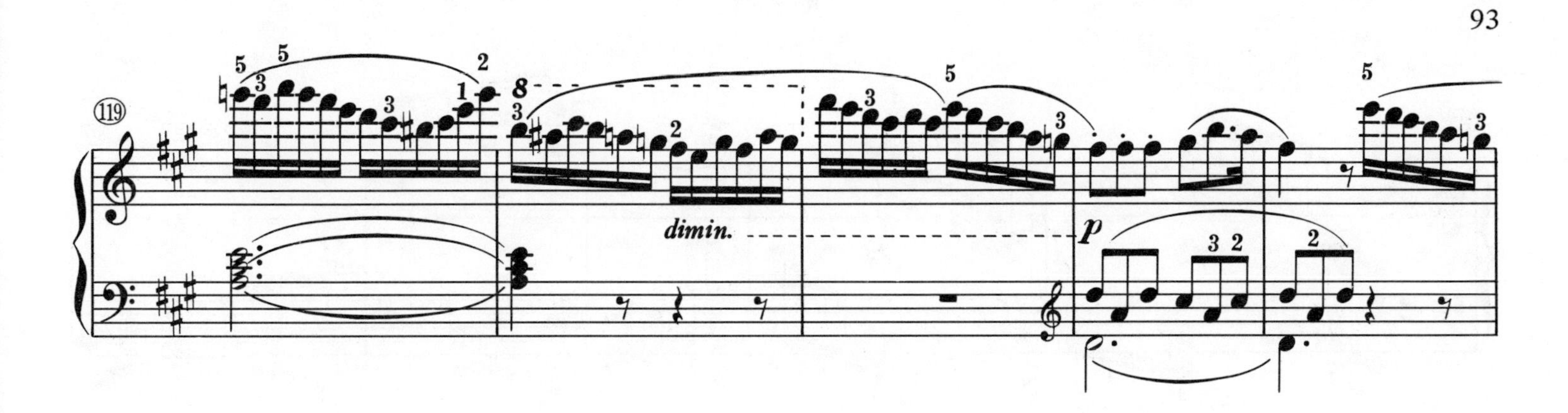
119
8
dimin.
p

124

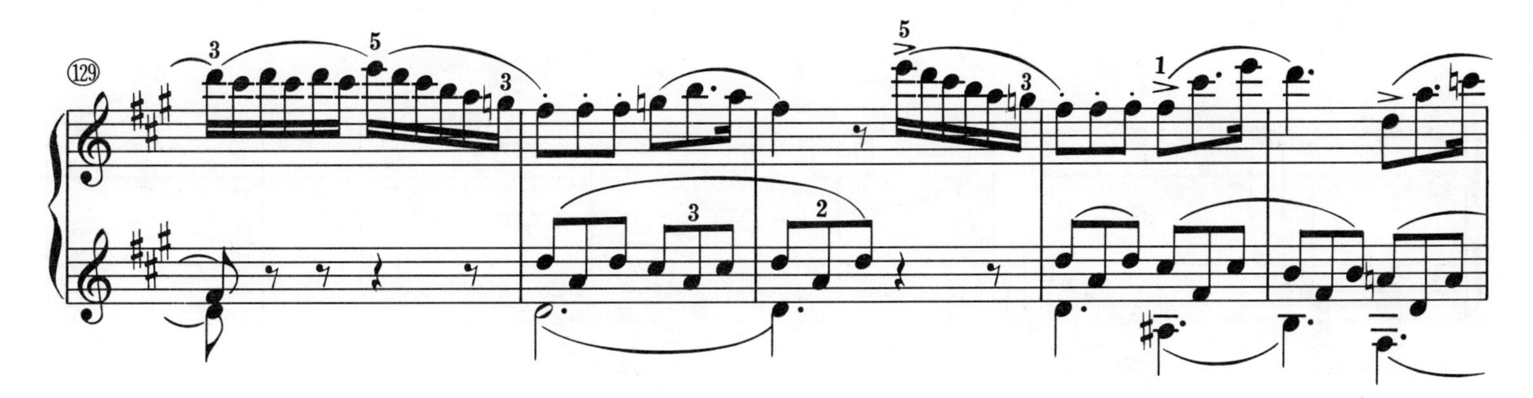
129

134
8

139
f legato
fz
fz

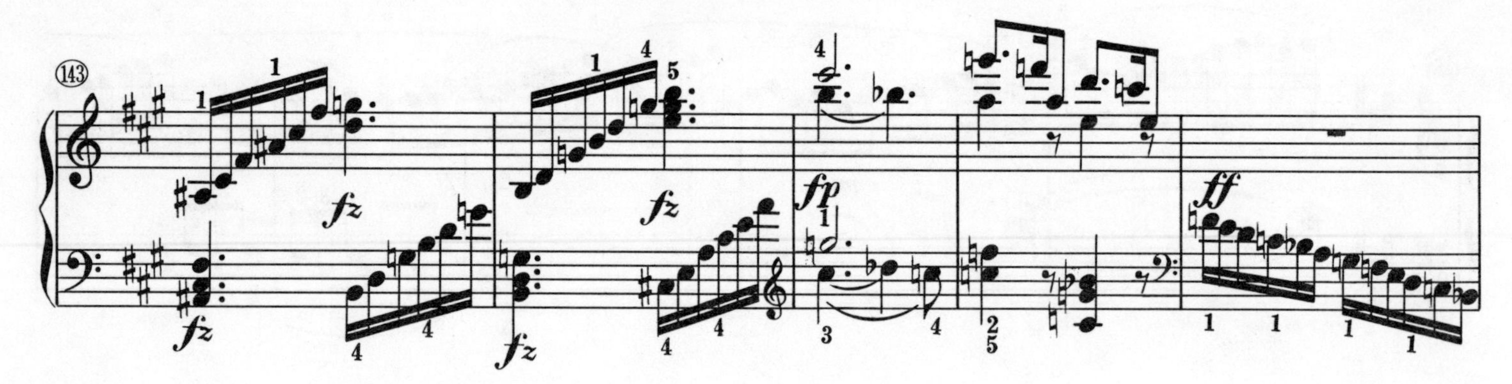
143
fz
fz
fz
fz
fp
ff

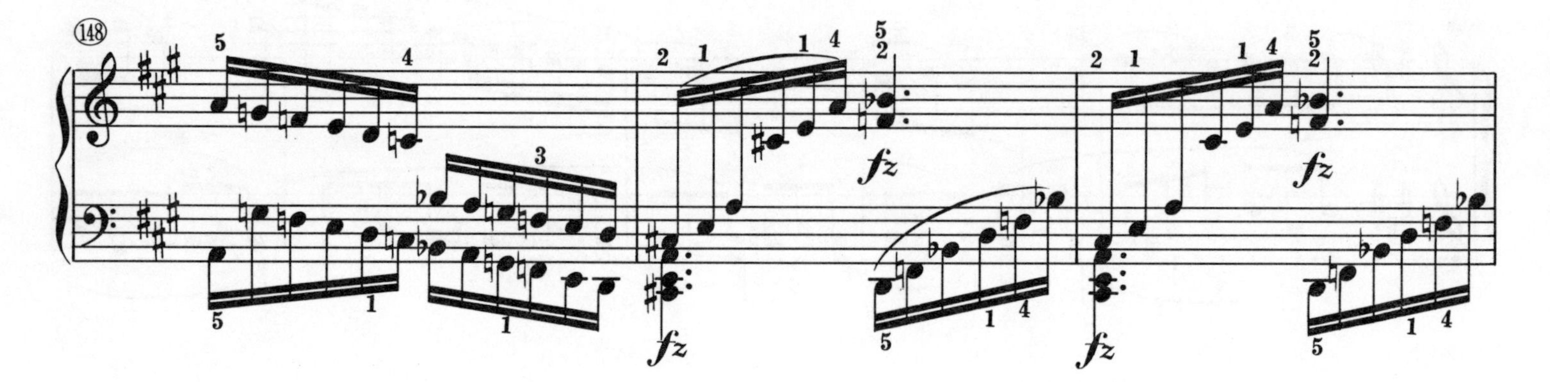
148
fz
fz
fz
fz

151
fz
fz
fp
p

157

164
p

171

176

180
p legato

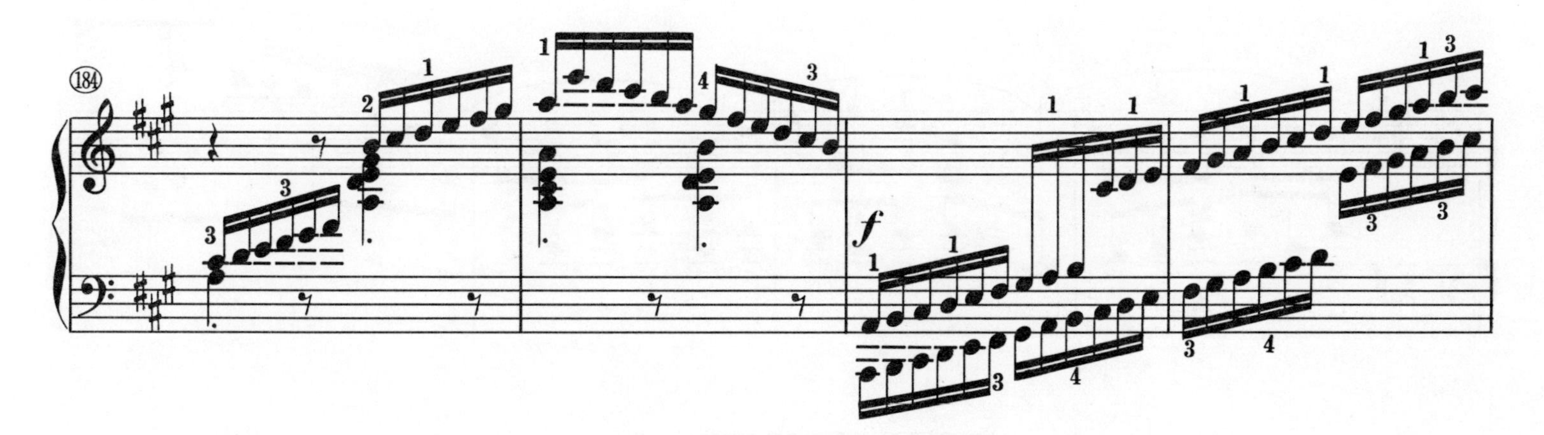
184

188

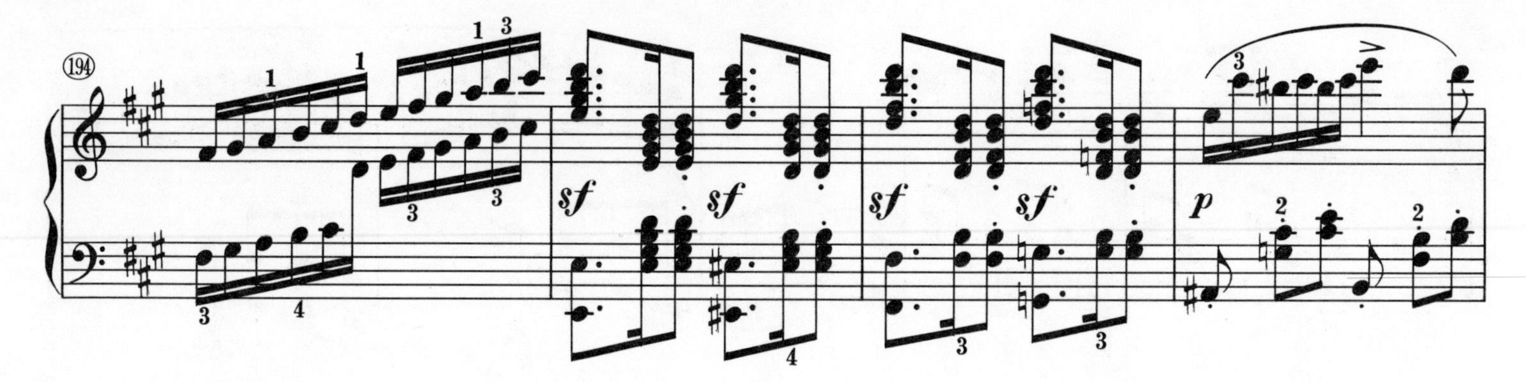
194
sf
sf
sf
sf
p

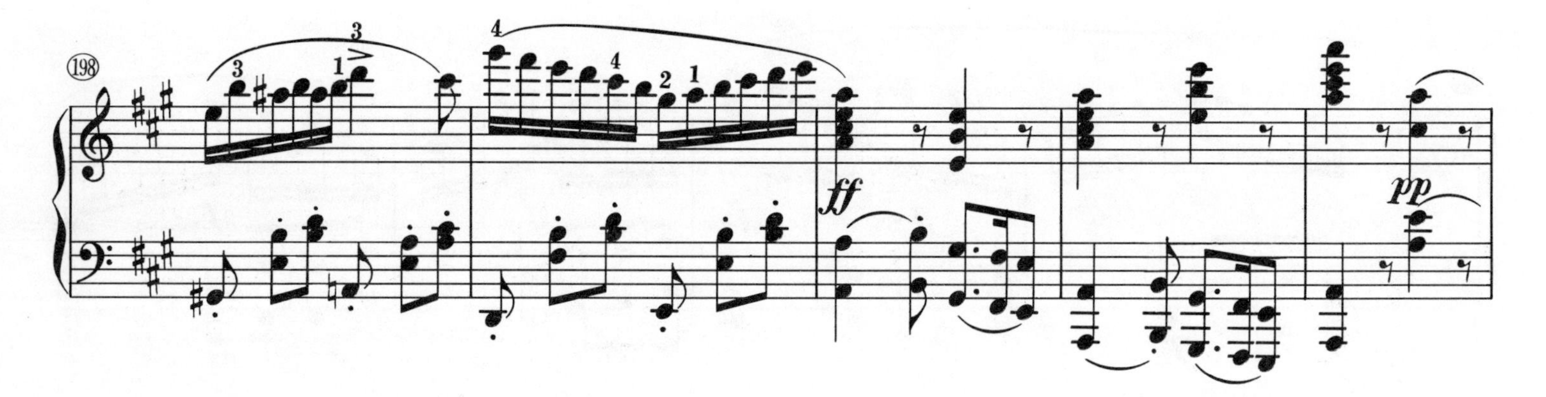
198
ff
pp

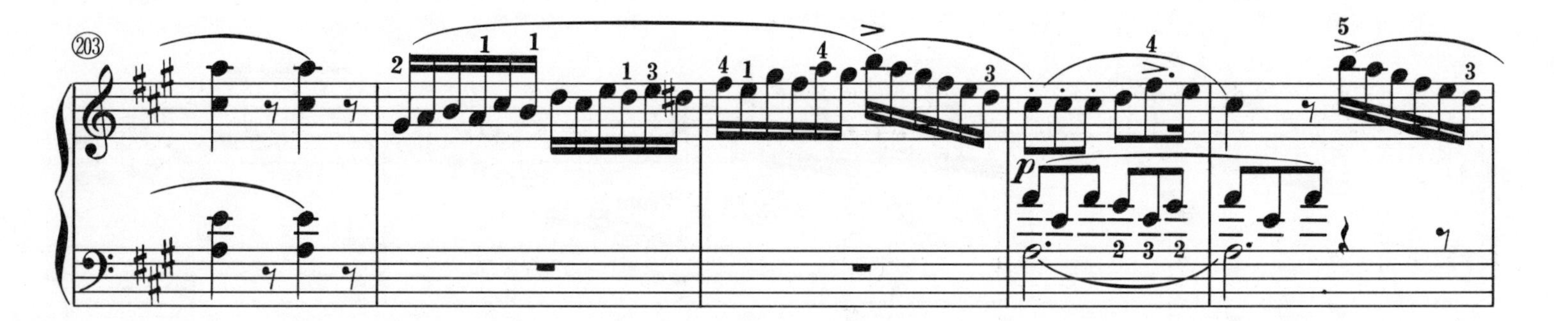
203
p

208

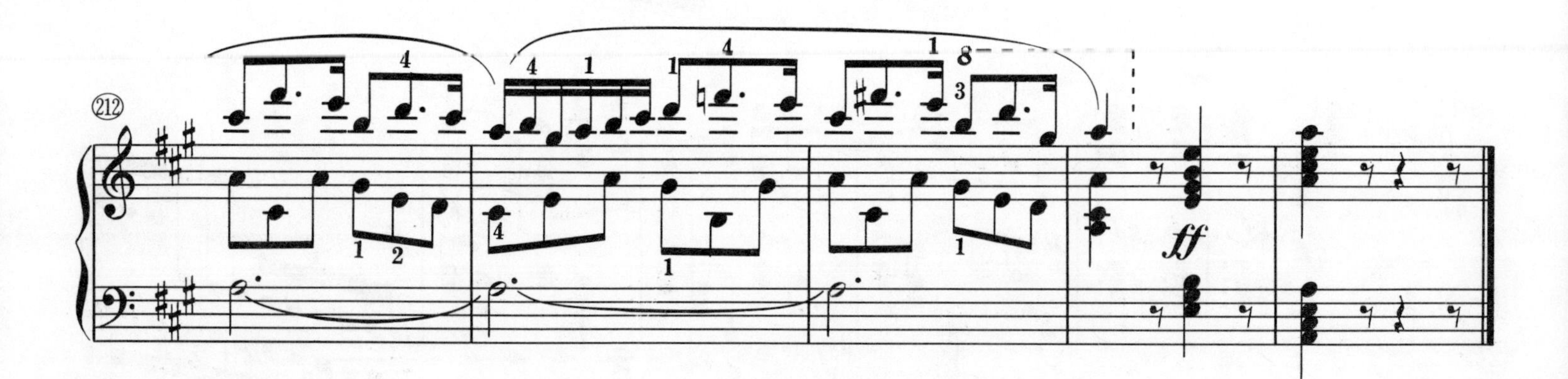
212
8
ff

SONATINA

(Op. 136, No. 1)

Carl Reinecke

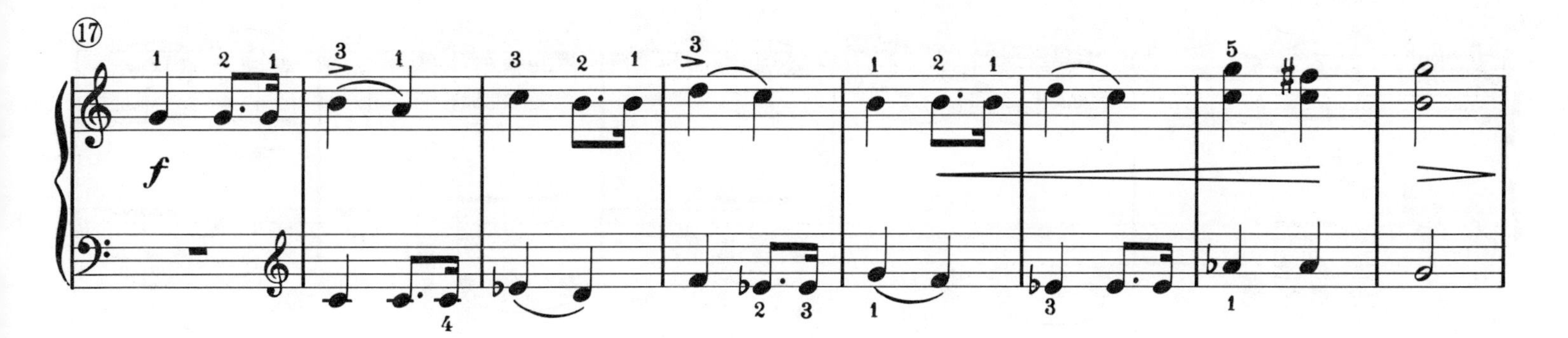

Andantino
p

f
p

Poco più lento
dolce

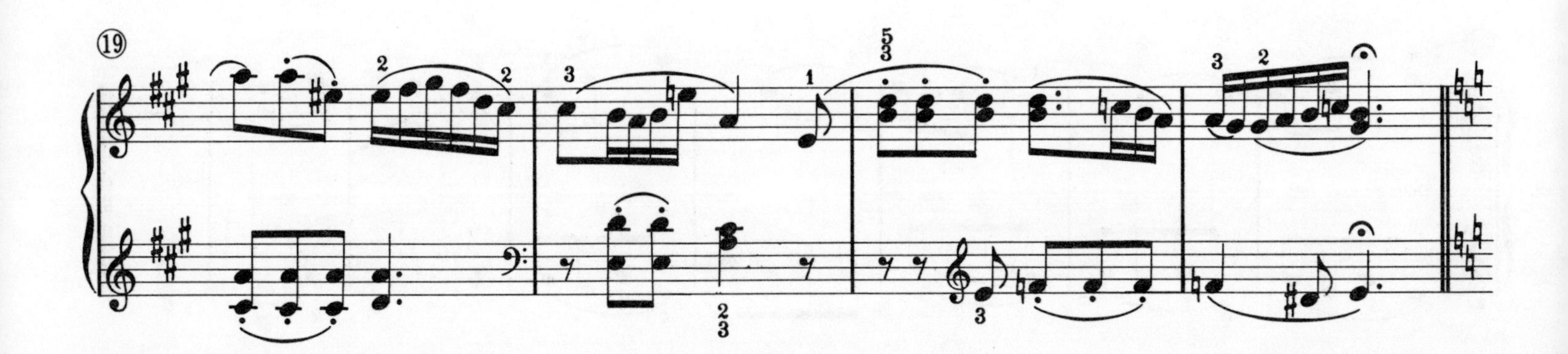

Tempo primo
p

(dim.)

Scherzino Vivace
p

mf

cresc.
f
p

Alla Polacca

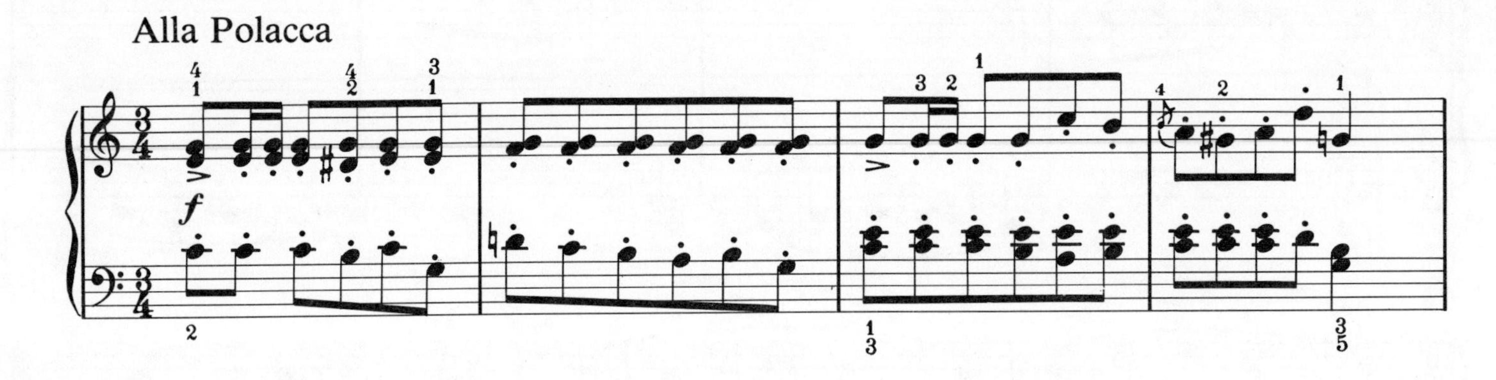

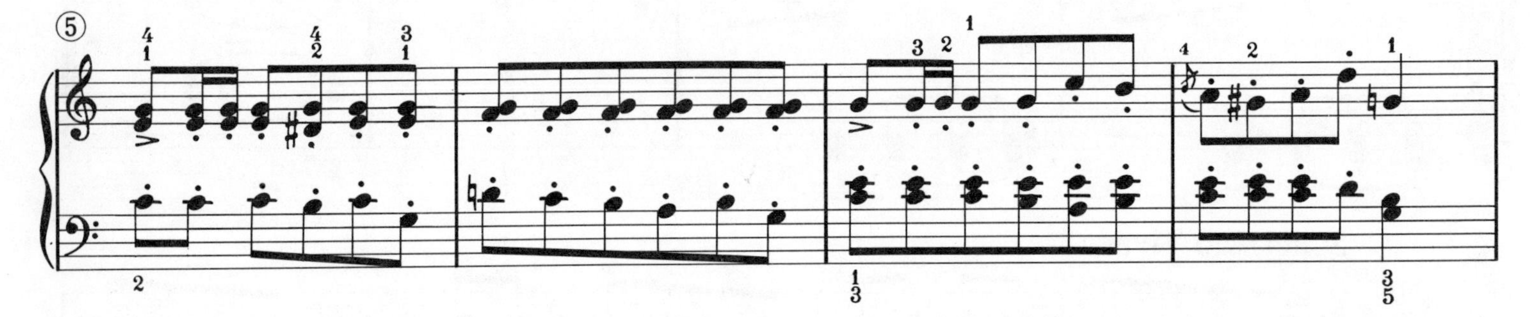

SONATINA
(Op. 207, No. 2)

Jacob Schmitt

Allegretto

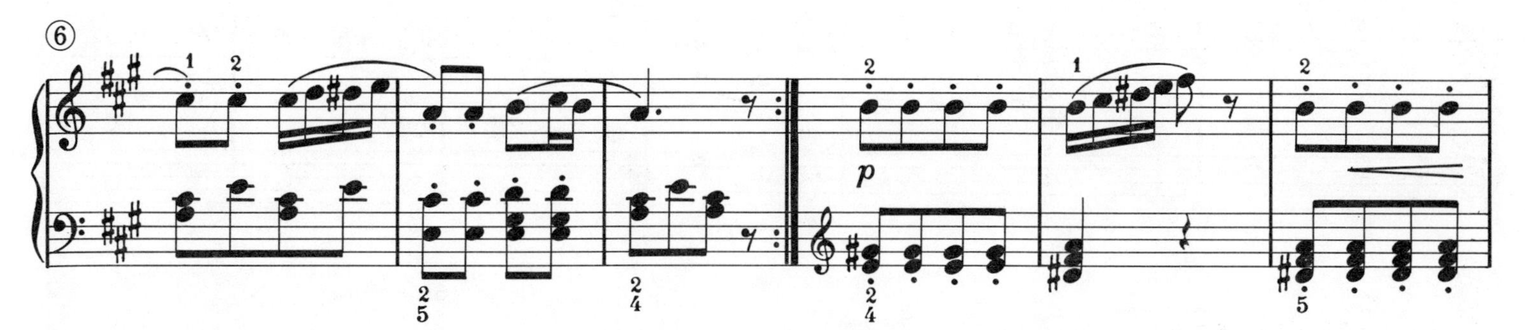

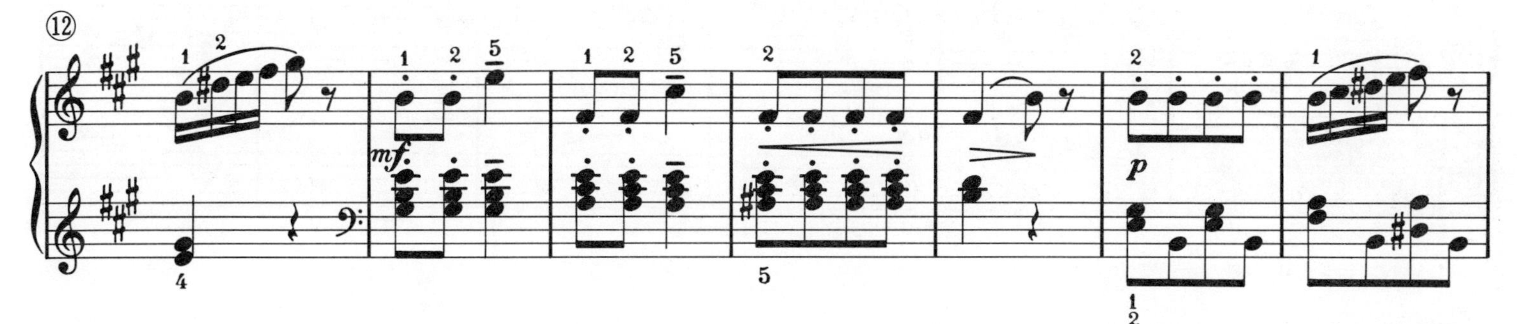

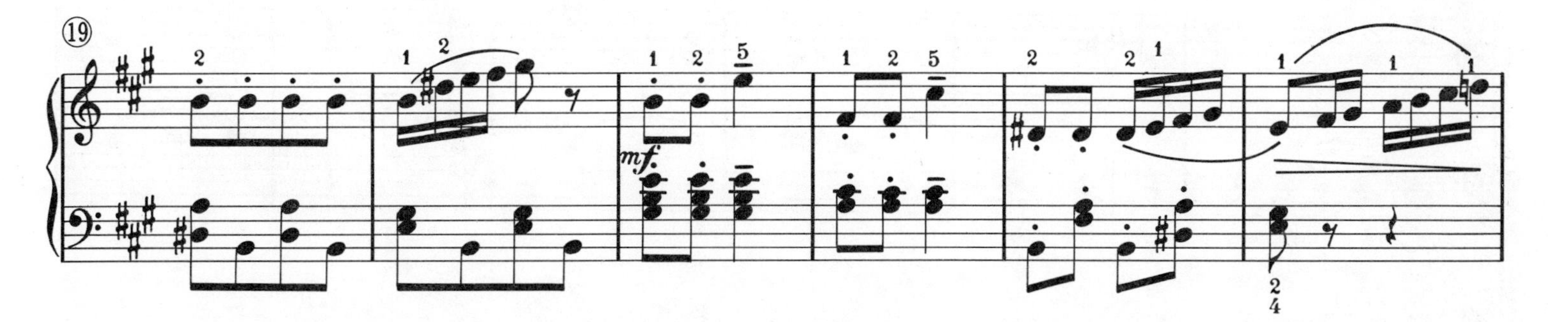

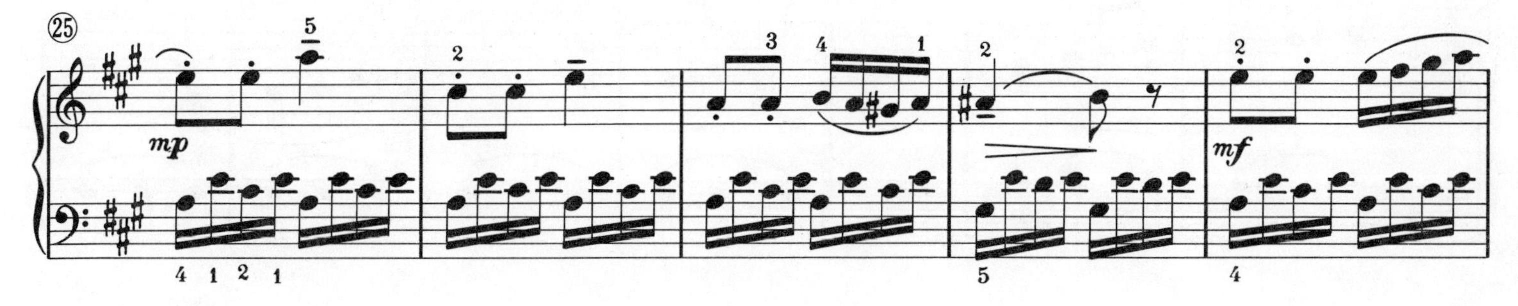

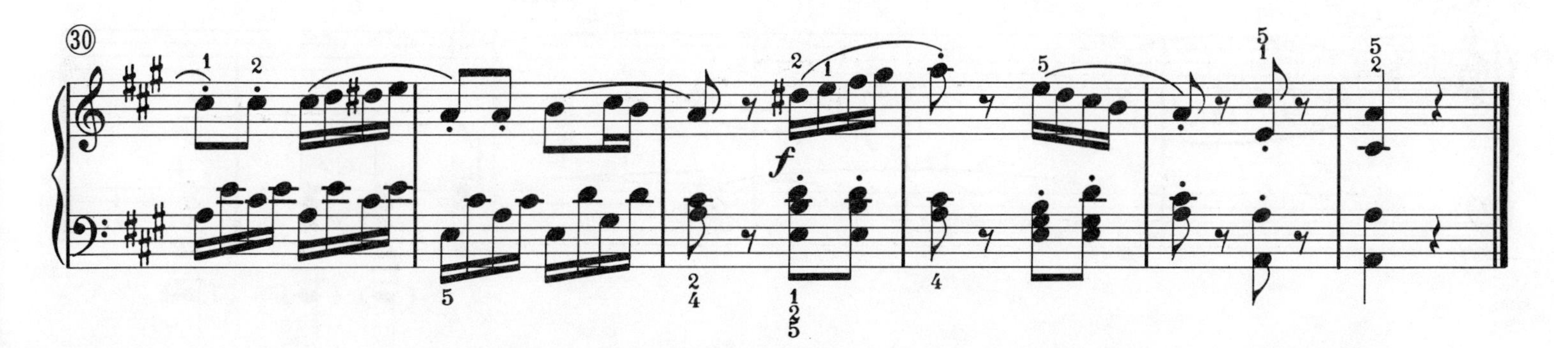

Andante

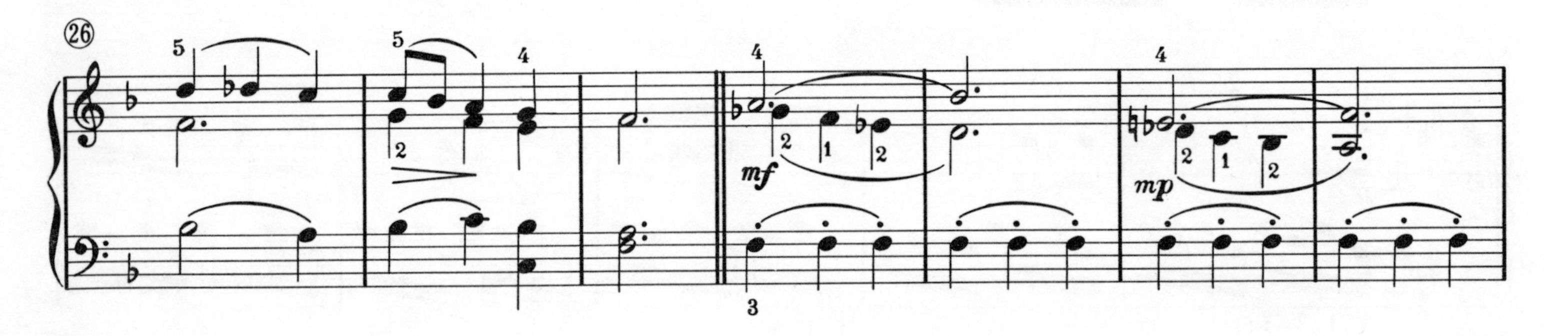

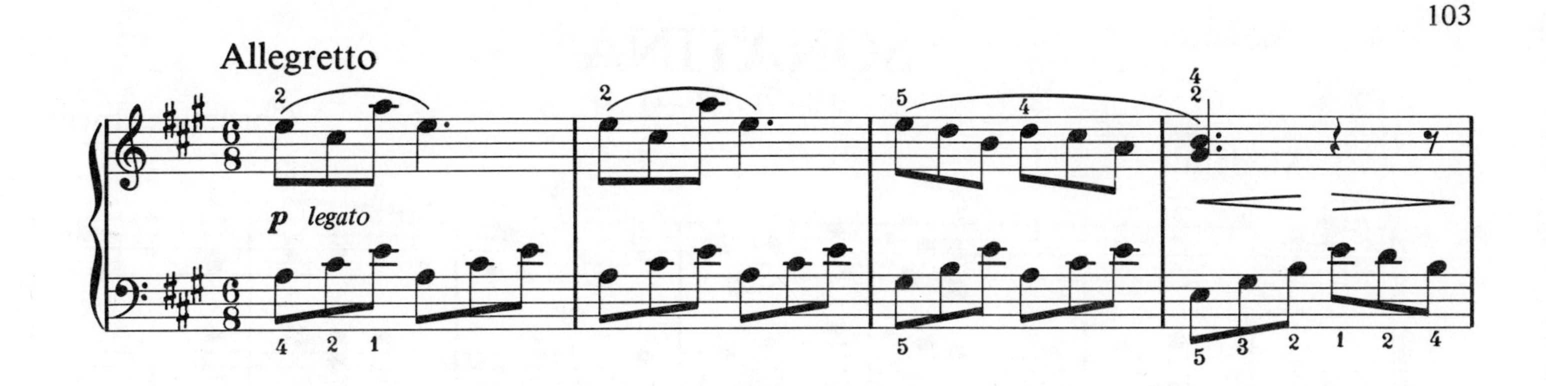
Allegretto
p legato

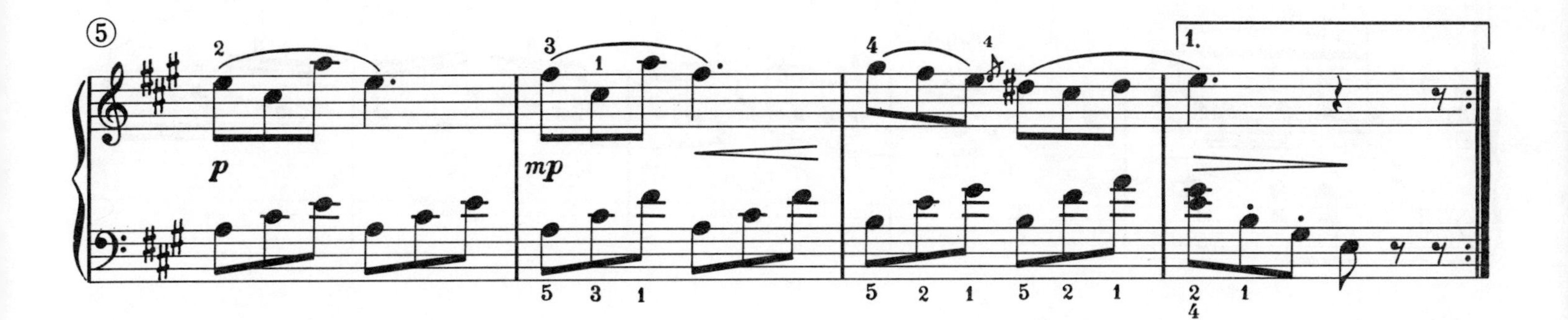
p
mp
1.

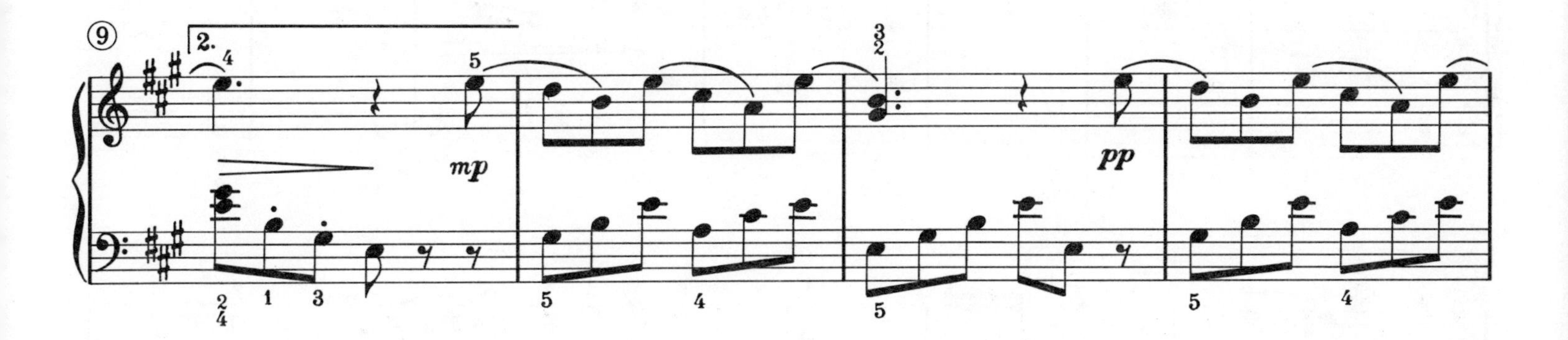
2.
mp
pp

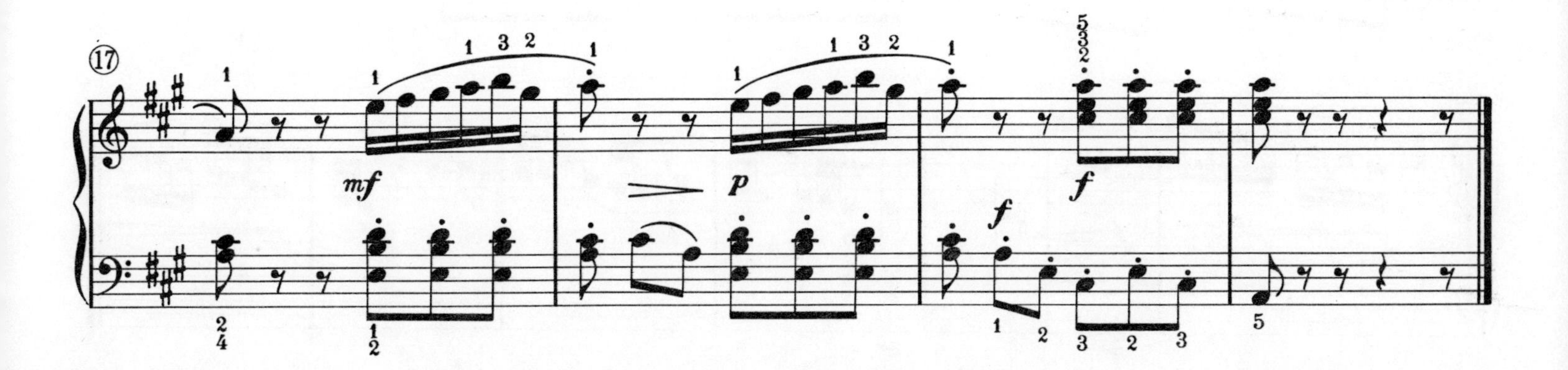
mf
p
f
f

SONATINA

(Op. 76, No. 2)

Cornelius Gurlitt

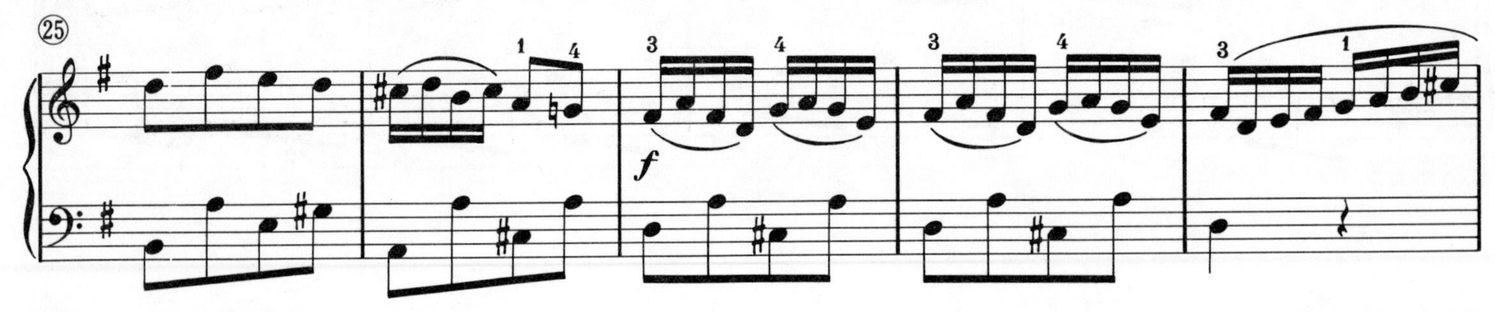

37
rit.

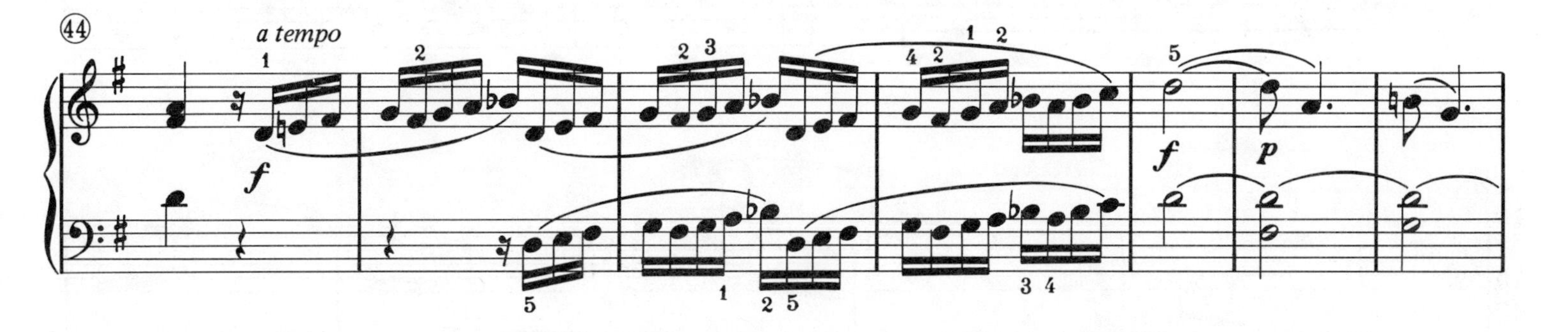
44
a tempo

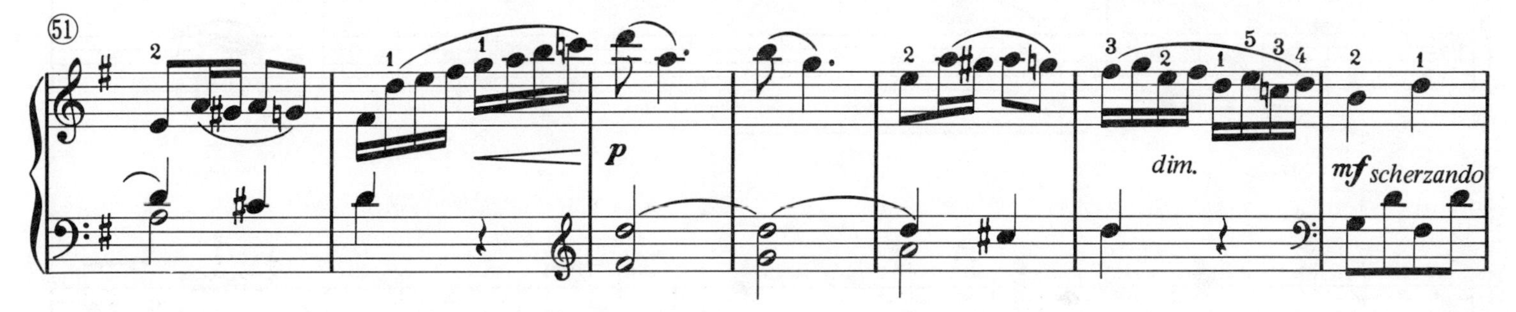
51
dim.
scherzando

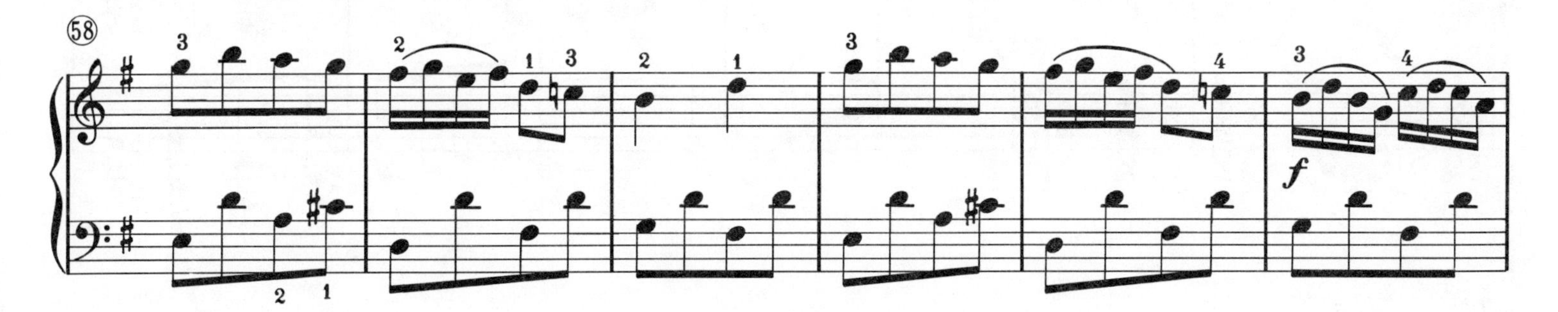
58

64

71

SONATA

Op. 7

Edvard Grieg

Allegro moderato

29

36
41
cresc. sempre

46

53

60
sosten.
a tempo
p dolce

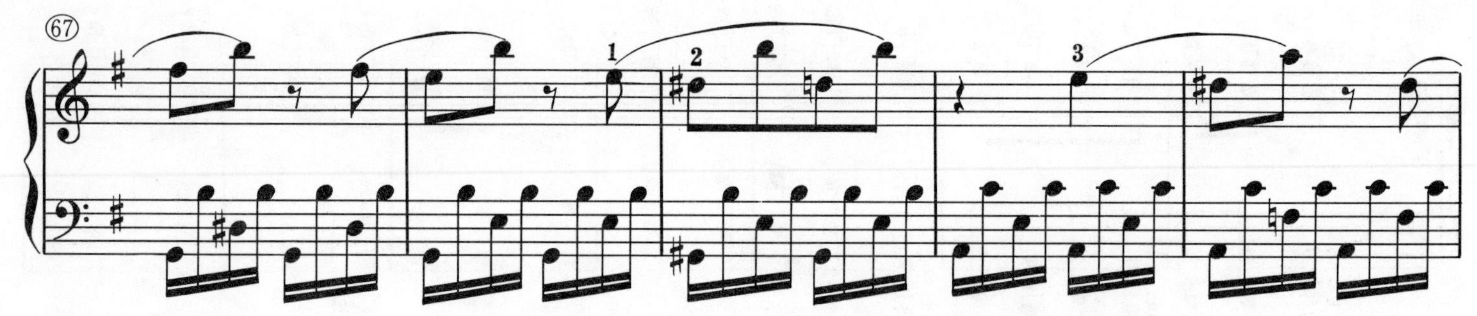

dim. e ritard.

ff

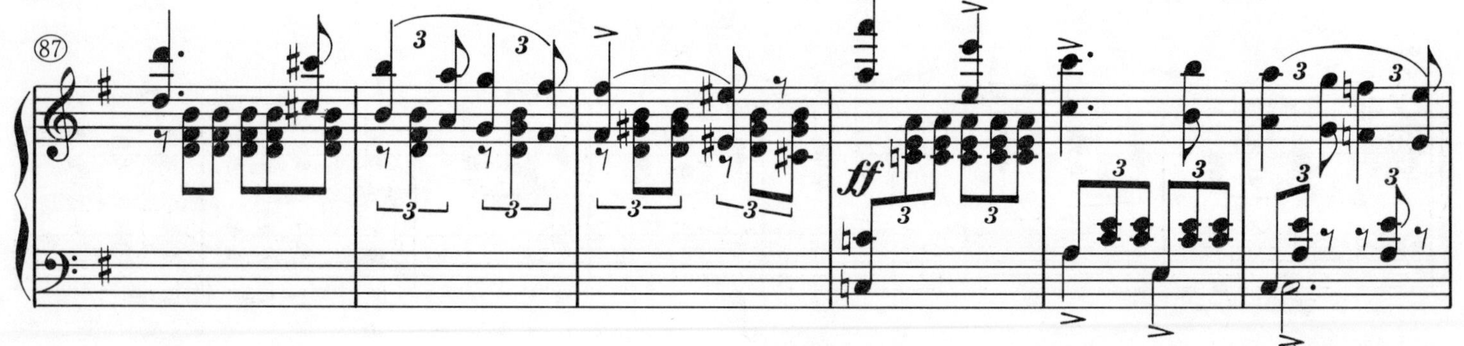
ff

p
sempre cresc.
il basso marcato

sempre cresc.

molto cresc. sempre

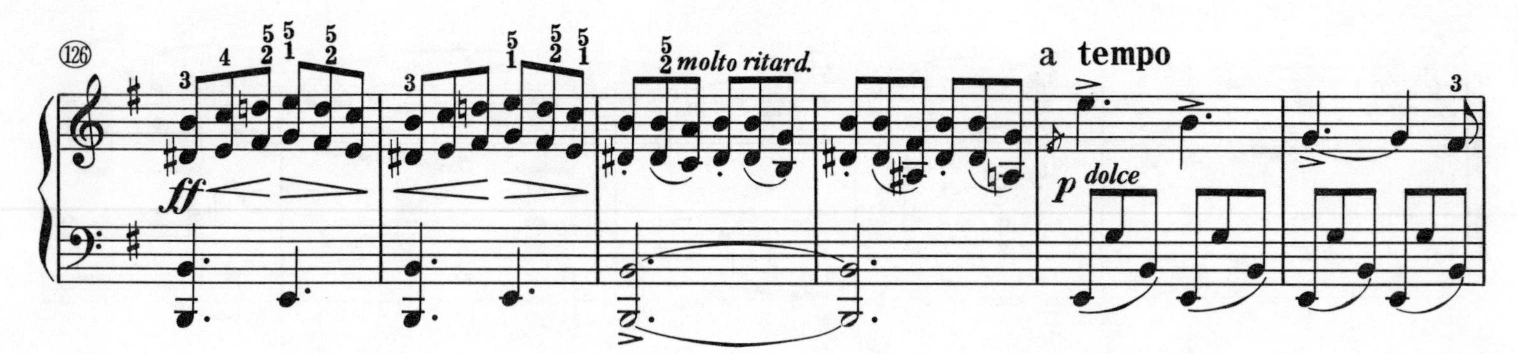
molto ritard.
a tempo
ff
p dolce

p
leggiero

cresc.
f
ff

più f

sosten.

161
3
3
p
p
ff

164
mf
cresc.

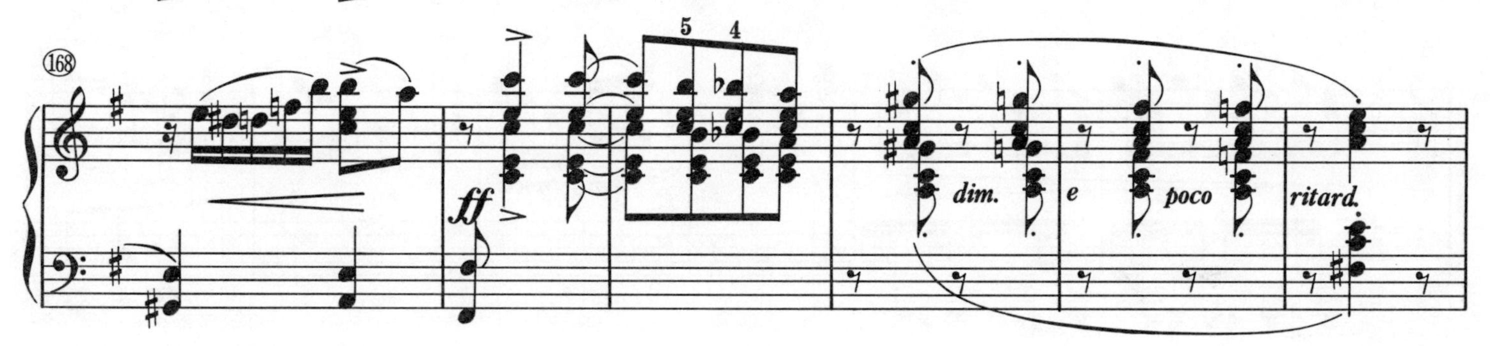
168
ff
5
4
dim.
e
poco
ritard.

174
a tempo
p
3

182
3
pp
5
3

189
poco ritard.
Allegro molto
3
2
p
1
2

194

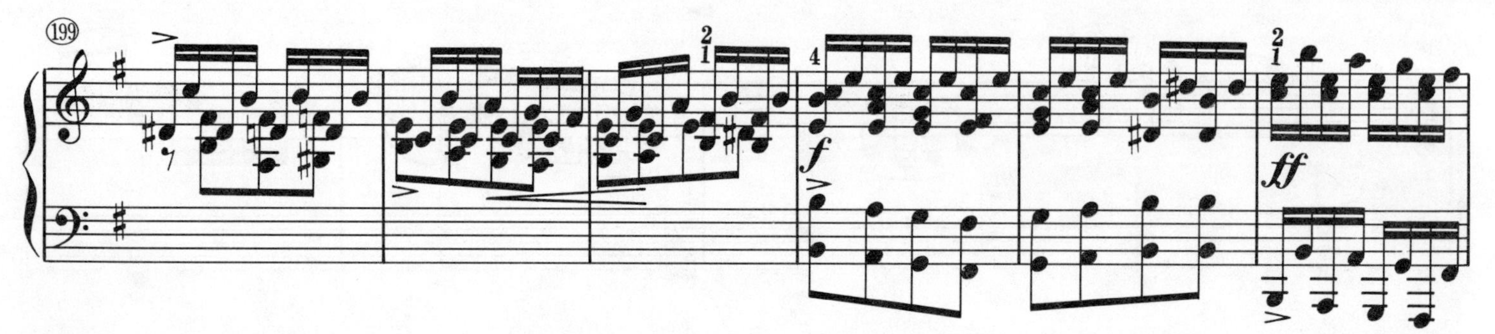
199
f
ff

205
ff
con fuoco

211
sf
sf
p
mf

217
cresc.
sf
sf
sf
molto cresc.

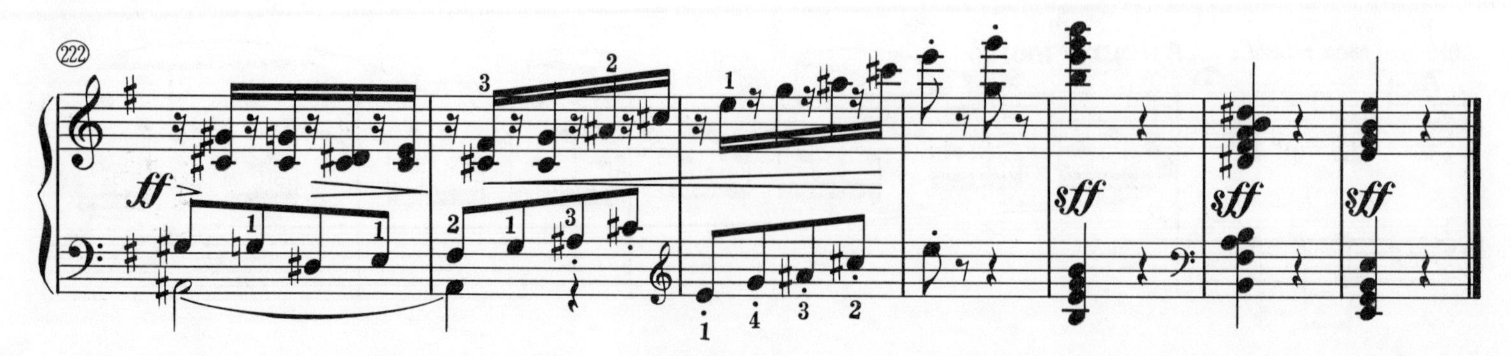
222
ff
sff
sff
sff

Andante molto
cantabile
p
con ped.

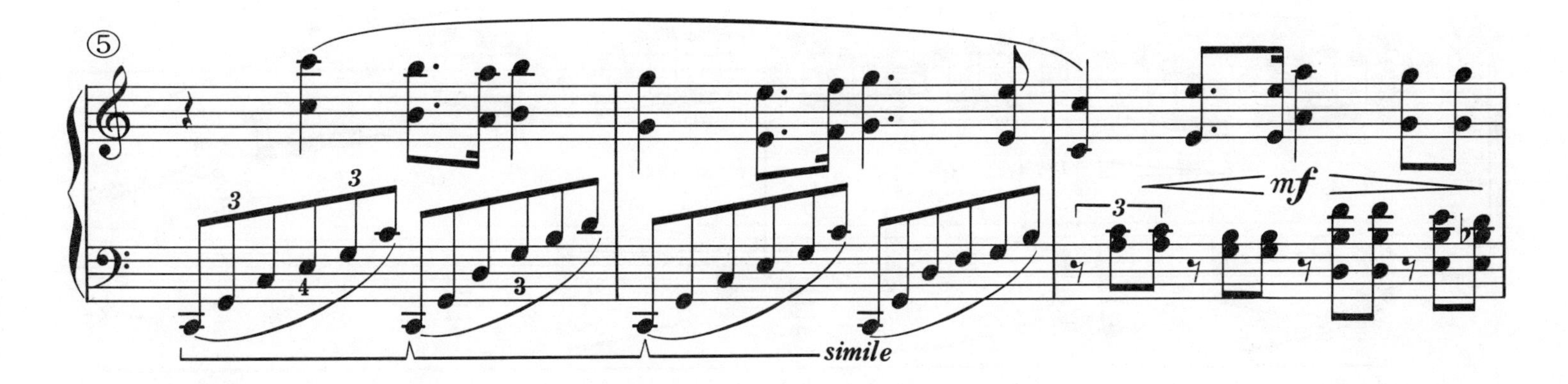
mf
simile

L'istesso tempo
cantabile

ff
p
ped. come sopra

ff

114

17
un poco più vivo
p

19
cresc.
cresc. molto

21
f
più f

24
ff
sf

26
ff

28

30
Tempo I
pp

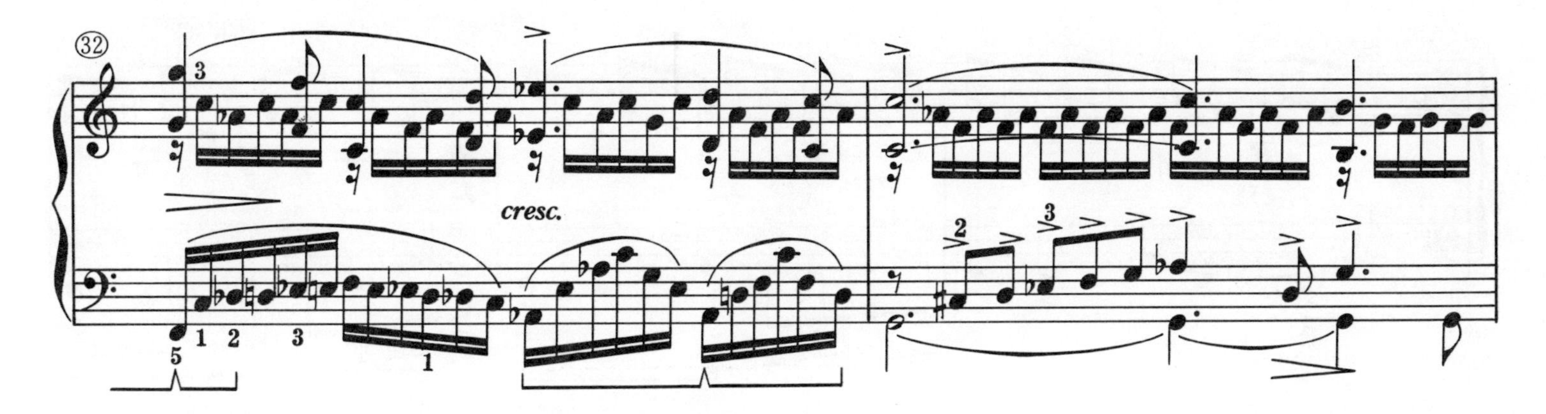
32
cresc.

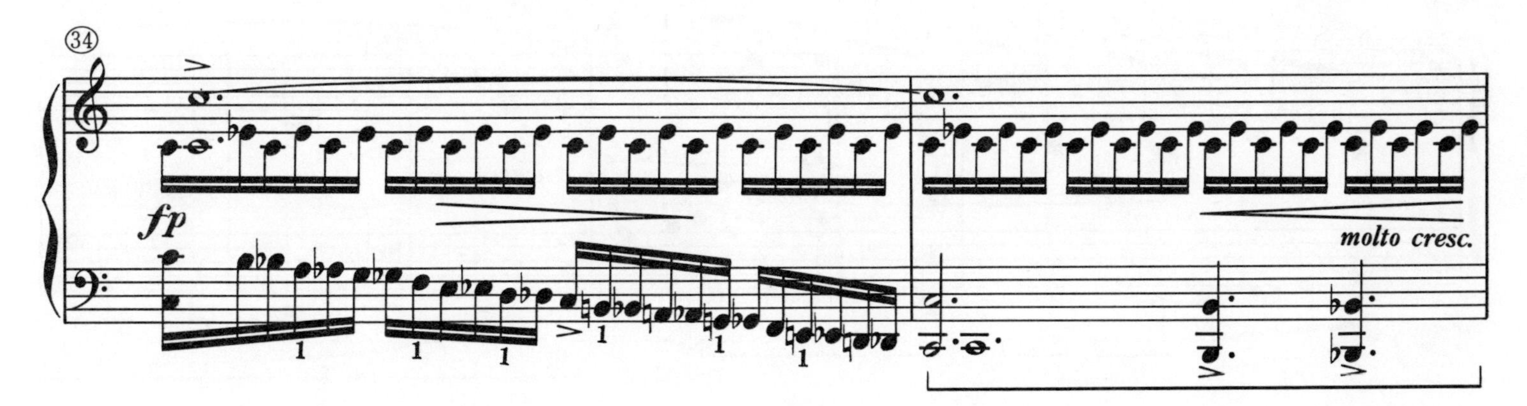
34
fp
molto cresc.

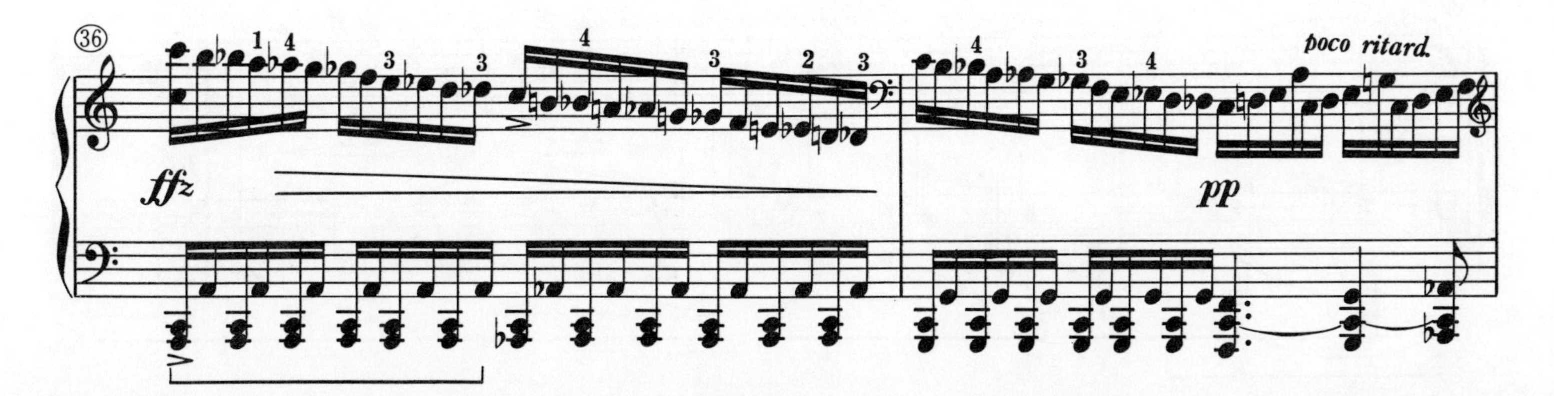
36
ffz
pp
poco ritard.

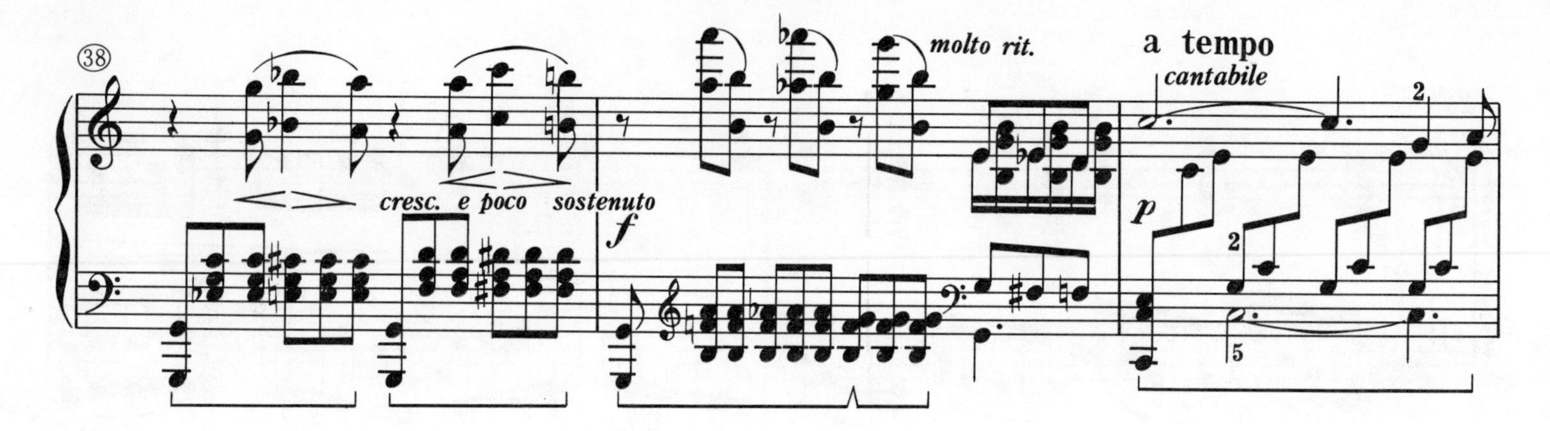
38
molto rit.
a tempo
cantabile
cresc. e poco sostenuto
f
p

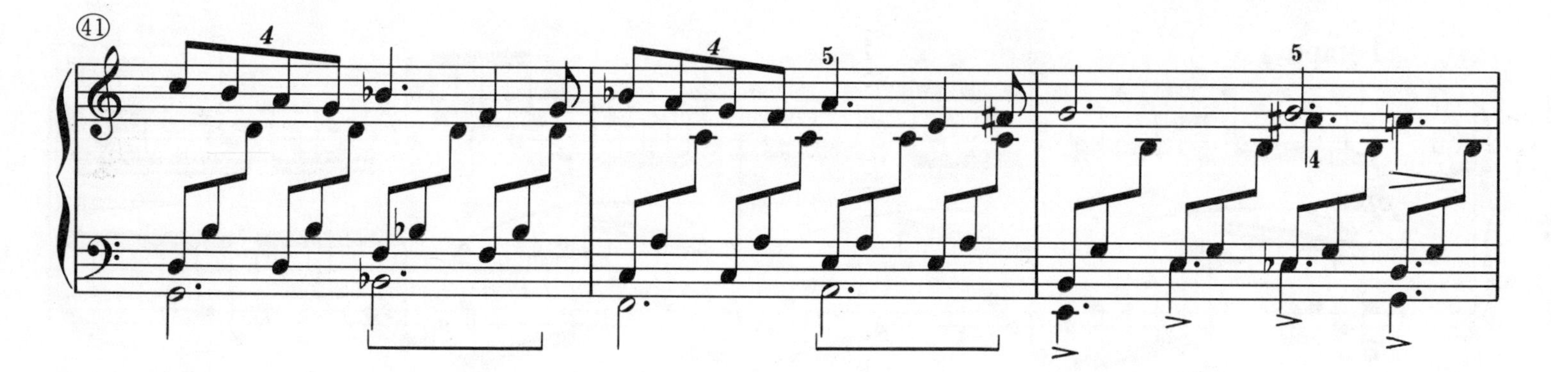
41

44
cresc.
f

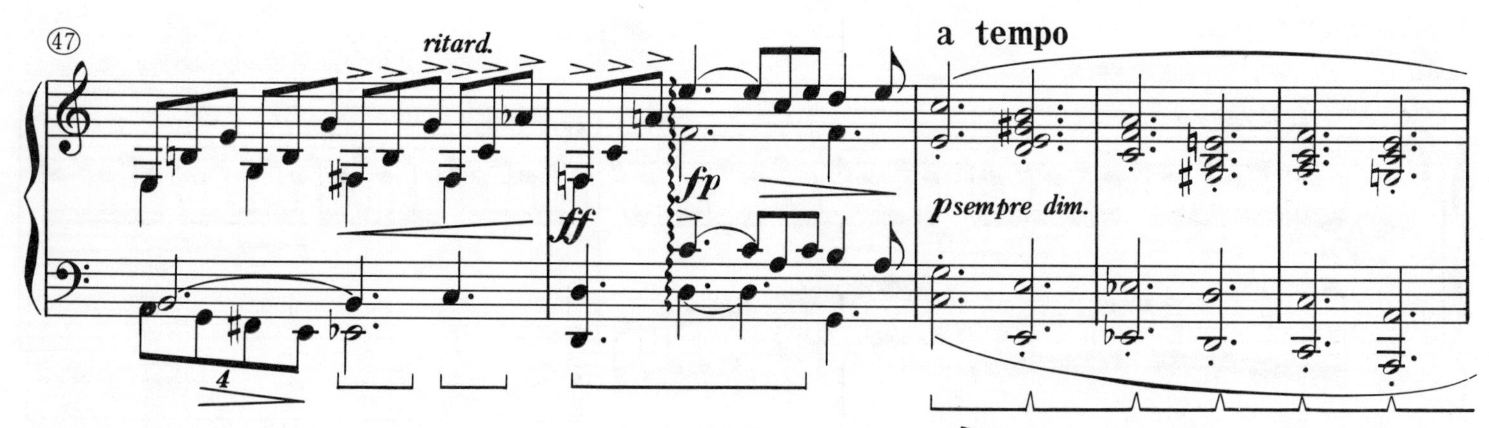
47
ritard.
a tempo
fp
ff
p sempre dim.

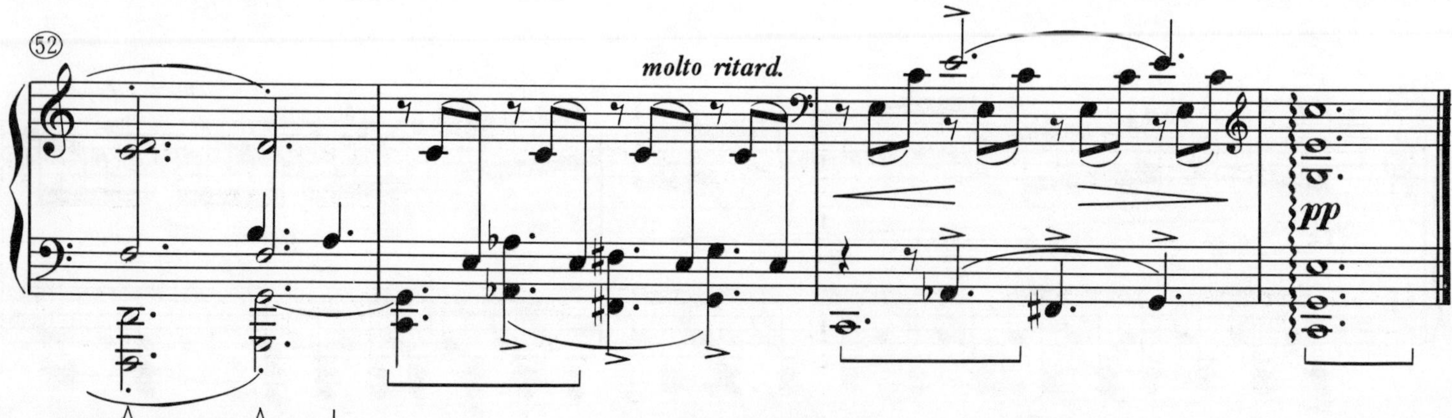
52
molto ritard.
pp

Alla Menuetto, ma poco Più lento
p
cresc.

ff
dim.

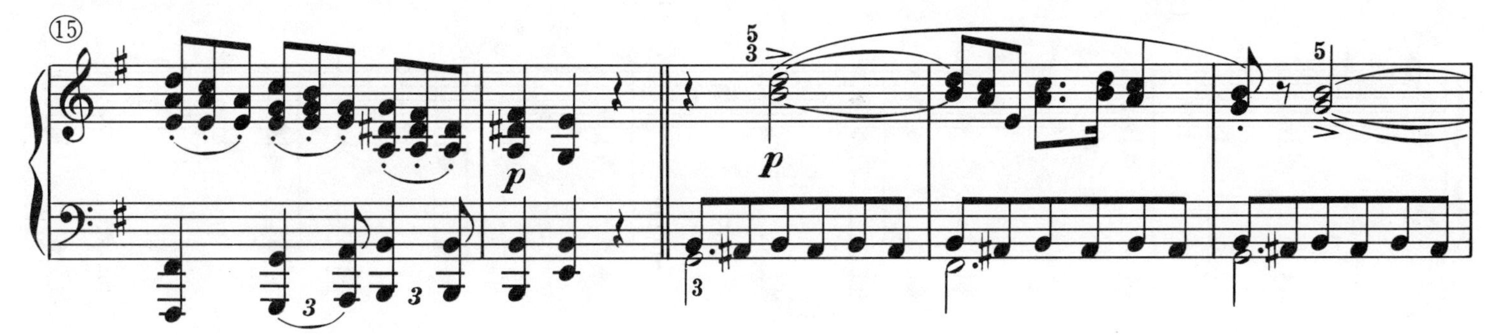
p
p

cresc.

ff

pesante
sf
ff

ritard.
a tempo
p

pp

p

p

pp

Finale

Molto allegro

12
p
poco a poco cresc.

17

22
ff

26

31
cresc.
f con fuoco

37
dim.

41
p
pp

47
pp
pp

55
mf

63
pp
mf

70
sf
f
sf

77

83

89
fp

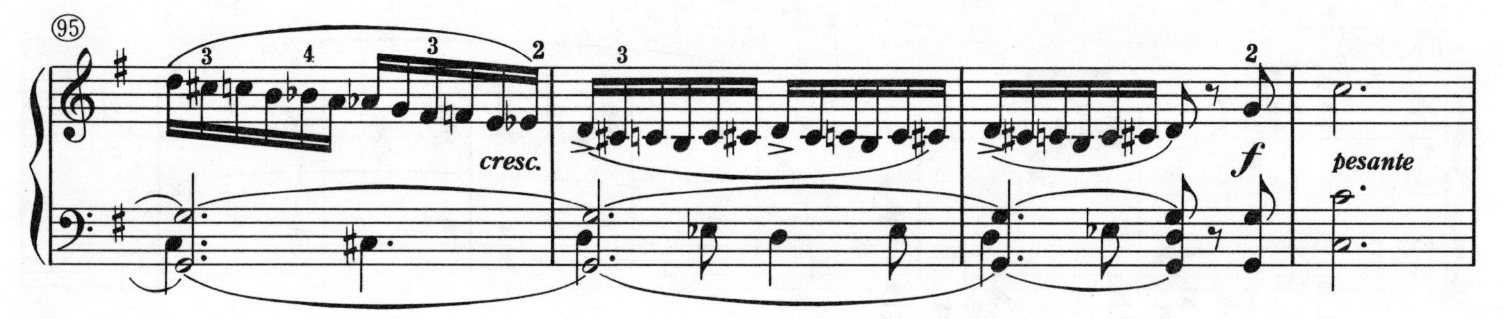
95
cresc.
f
pesante

99
sf
ff

106

111

115

122
pp

127

134
pp
cresc.
sempre

141
cresc.
f

146
pp

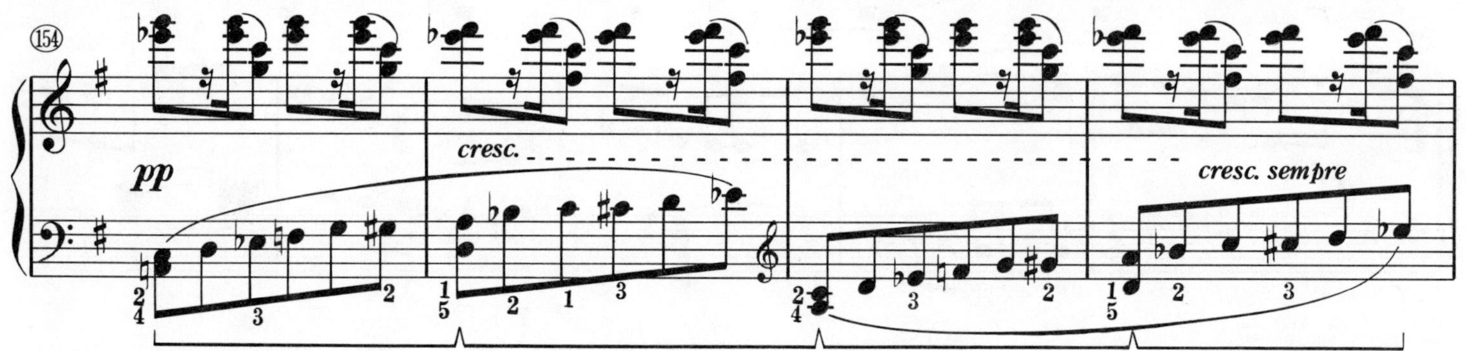
pp
cresc.
cresc. sempre

sosten.

a tempo
ff sempre

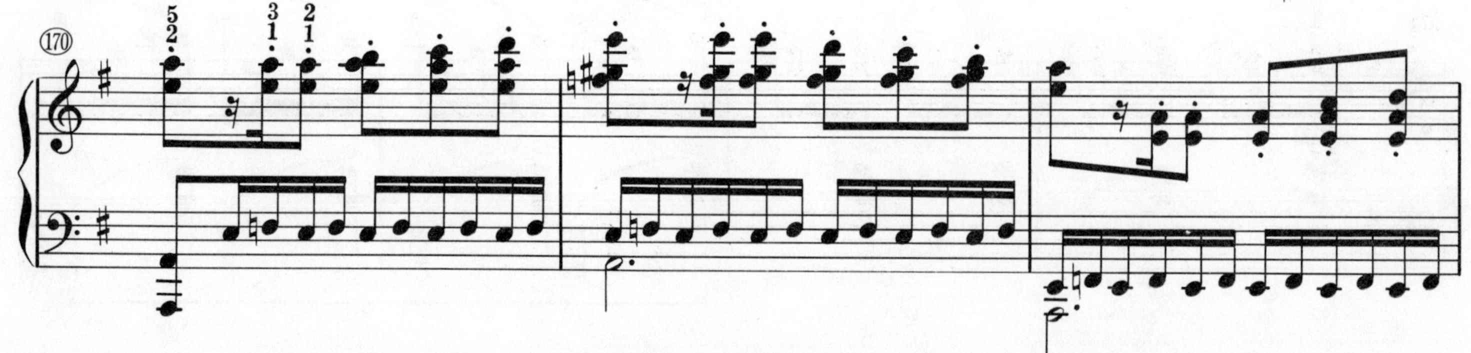

173

177
fp
sf

182
mf
cresc.

186
ff

190

194
sosten.
sf
sosten.
sf
p

199
pp
poco rit.
pp

205
(a tempo)
p
p

211
p
staccato sempre
cresc. sempre

217

222
ff

226
p

231
cresc.

236
8
dim.

240
pp

246
mp
pp

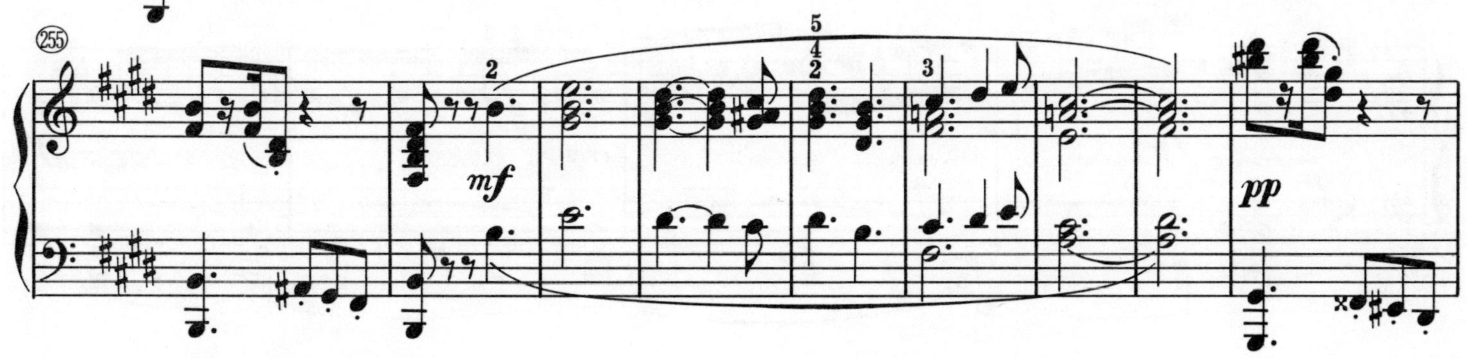
255
mf
pp

264
f

271

279
dim.
p

285

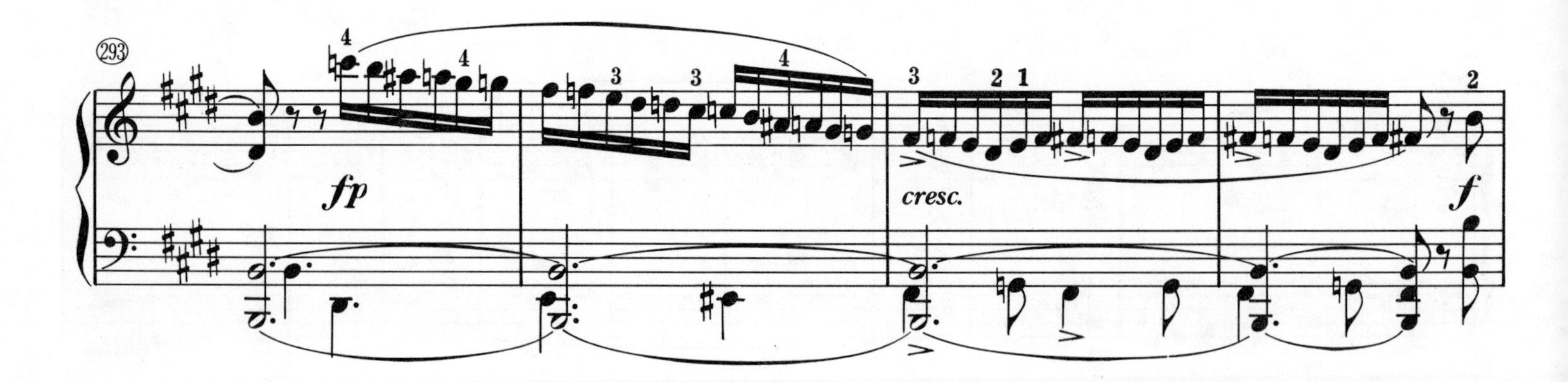
293
fp
cresc.
f

297
sf
ff

305
2

311
sosten.
fff
sempre grandioso

317

324
sosten.

331
ritard.
Presto

337
8

SONATA No. 3

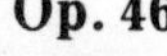

Op. 46

I

Allegro con moto

Dmitri Kabalevsky

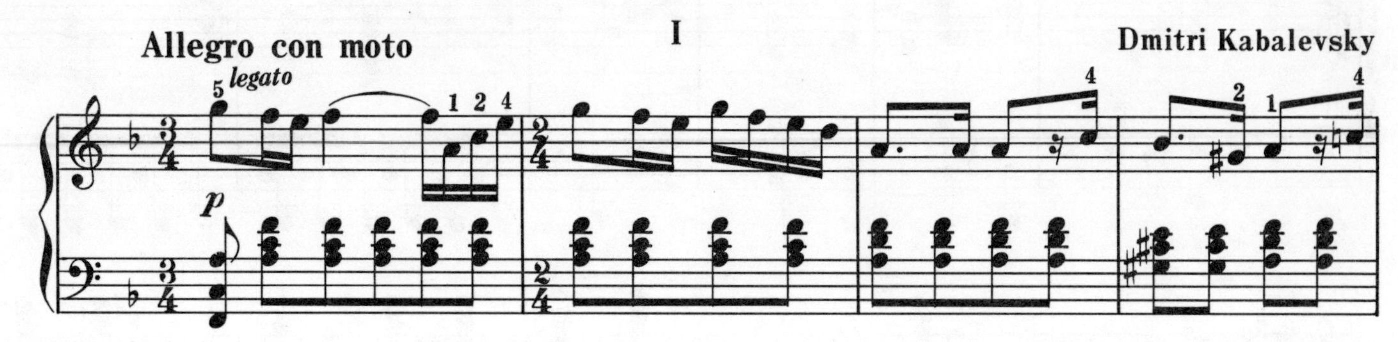

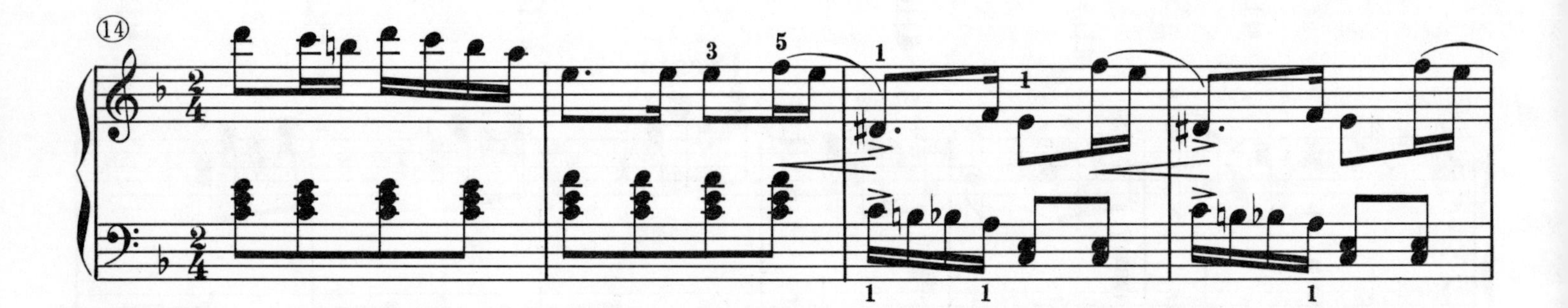

22
poco a poco cresc.

27

31
f
p sub.

35
f sub.
p sub.
cresc.

39
ff

43
(non rit.)

L' istesso tempo
49
cantando
p

56
legato

63
poco rit.
a tempo
mp

70
più f
poco - - - a - - - - - poco - - - cresc.

76
poco agitato
f

82
marcato

88

94
poco
a
poco
dim.

99
poco rit.
più
tranquillo
a tempo
dolce
p leggatissimo

105
espress.

111

117
rit.
molto

Più mosso, Con agitazione
pp secco e marcato
cresc.
cen
do
ff
pp
cresc.

158
f
8

164
sub.p
poco marcato

170

176
più f

182
cresc.

188
marcatissimo
5
4
1

194
sf
sf
sf
ff

200
f
f con fuoco
207
poco
a
poco

213
cresc.
cen
do

219

225
ff
meno f
e
cresc.

231
molto
ff
sff
sff
sff

238
sff
sff
sff
meno f
e
cresc.
molto

245
rit
molto
ff

Tempo I
252
legato
p

poco cresc.

262
p

266

270
mf

275
f
meno
f sempre cresc.

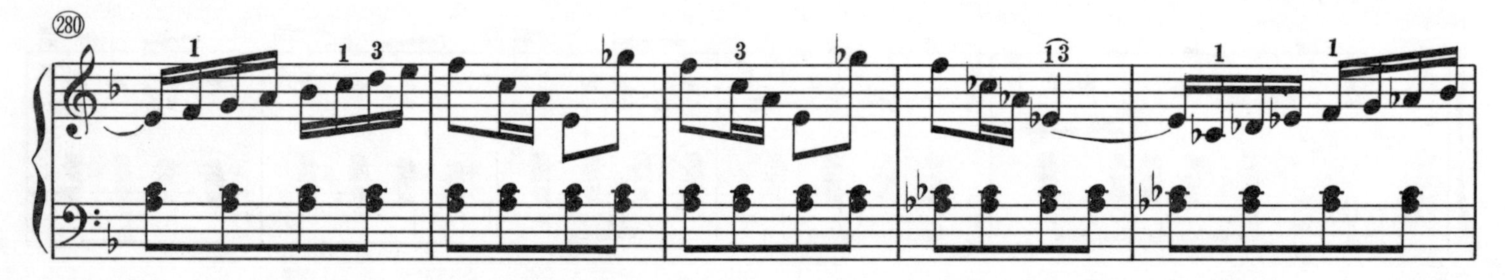
280

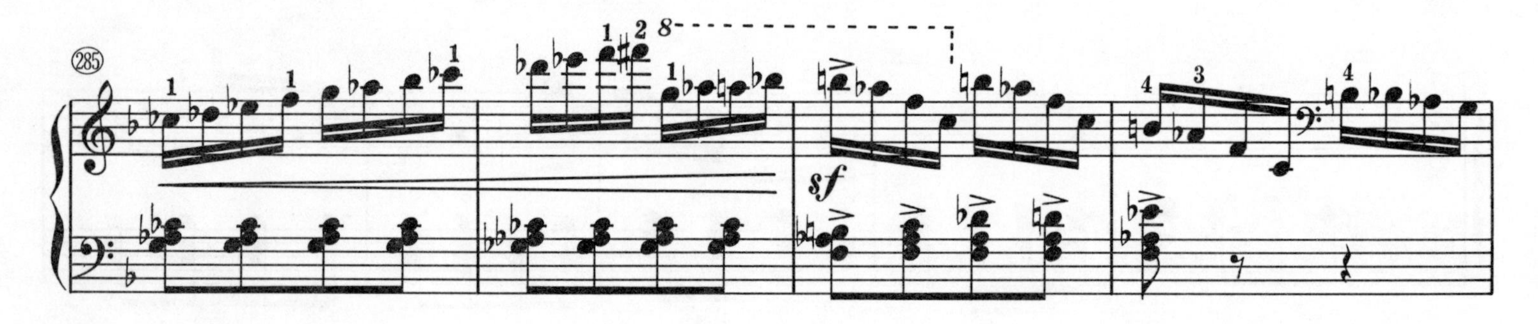
285
sf

289
f marcato

295
tenutissimo
ff

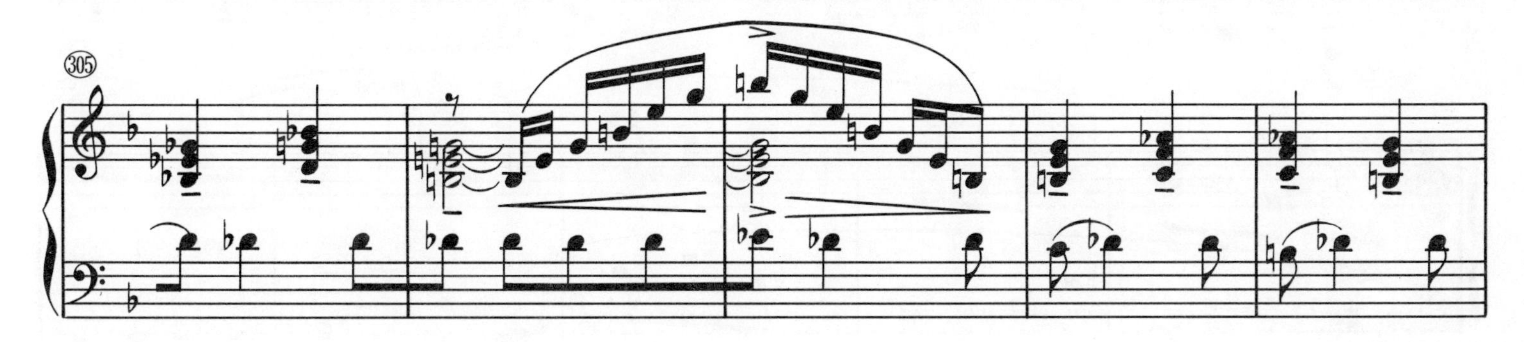
305

310

316
rit

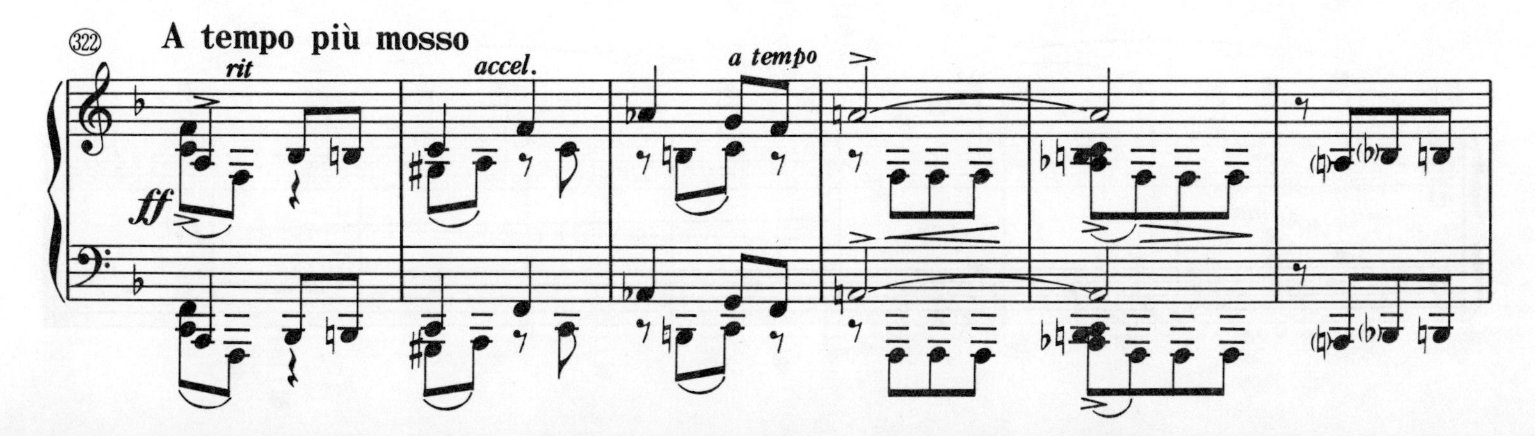
322
A tempo più mosso
rit
accel.
a tempo
ff

328
333
poco
a
poco
dim.
338
poco
rit.
a tempo
p
poco
cresc.
343
mp
348
p
dim.
al
Ped.
353
fine
pp

II

Andante cantabile
mf legato

pp

mp pp
mf sonoro

mp

p dolce
pp

poco - - - - - - a - - - - - - - - - poco - - - - cresc.

35
f
mf
espress.

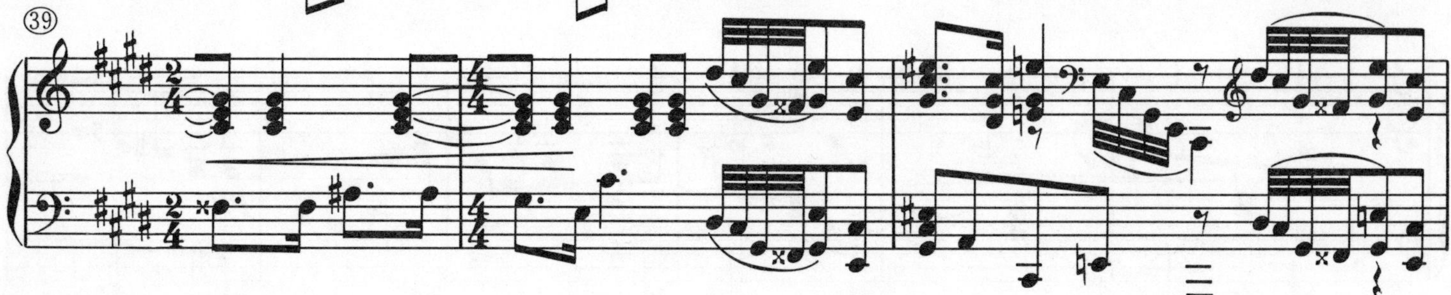
39

42
poco a poco cresc.

45

50
poco ritard.
mf

Tempo I
54
sonoro e candando

58
mp
poco rit.
62
p dolce
dim.
Poco meno mosso
pp
66
mp
rit.
a tempo (meno mosso del tempo I)
p
ff
71
p legato
pp
p legato
Ped.
76
f
mp
poco a poco

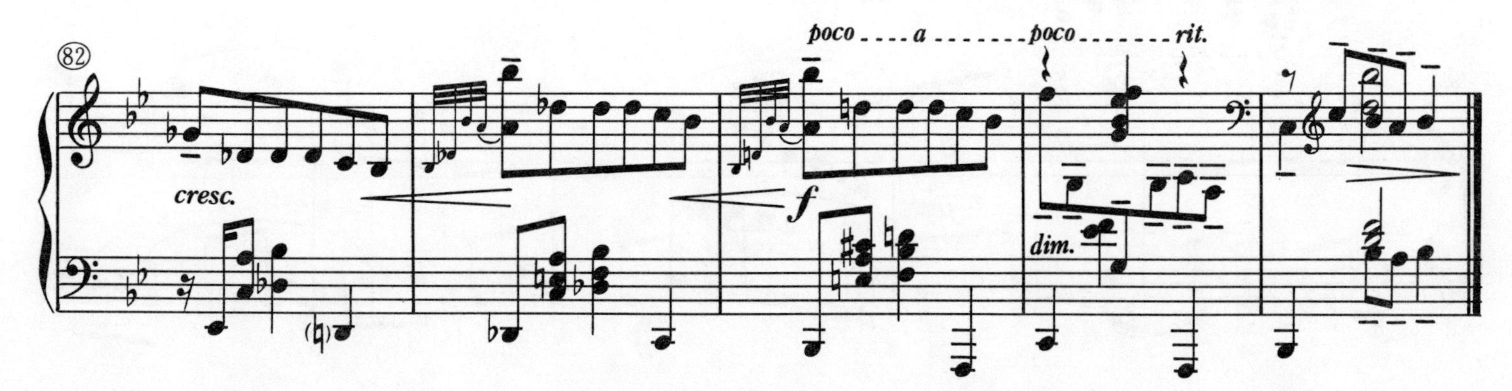
82
cresc.
poco a poco rit.
f
dim.

III

Allegro giocoso
pp sotto voce

7
poco cresc.

14
p

20
p

27
pp
legg.
8

33
8
p

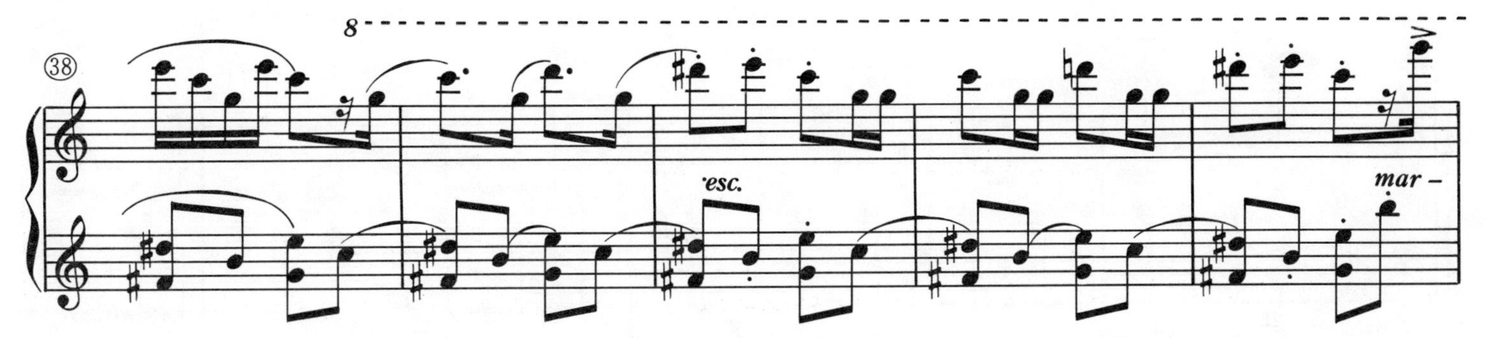
38
8
cresc.
mar –

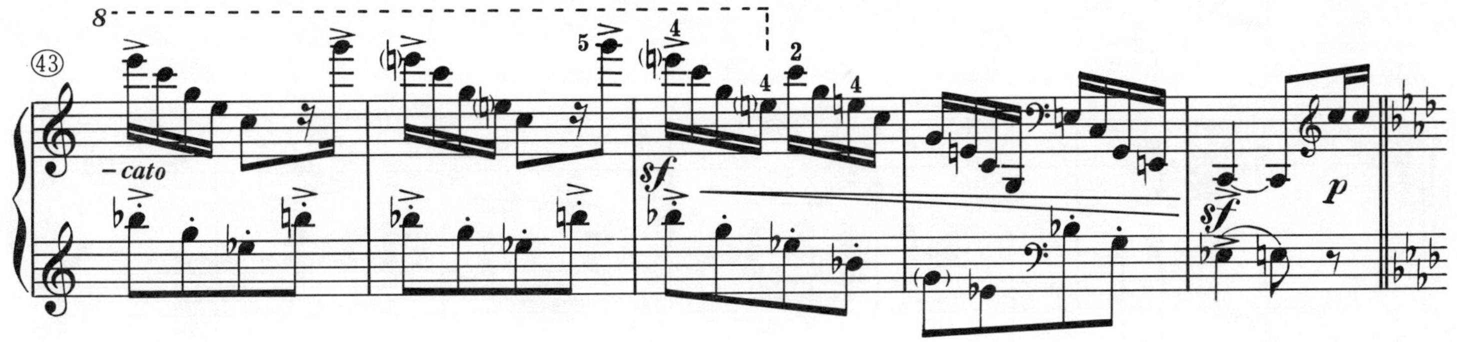
43
8
– cato
sf
p

48
p

53

57
pp

61
cresc.
f con brio

66

73

79
ff
f

85

91

99
cresc.

Pochissimo più mosso
(♩=♩)
107
ff marcato

113

119
7
7

122
7

125

131
secco
sf p sub.

136

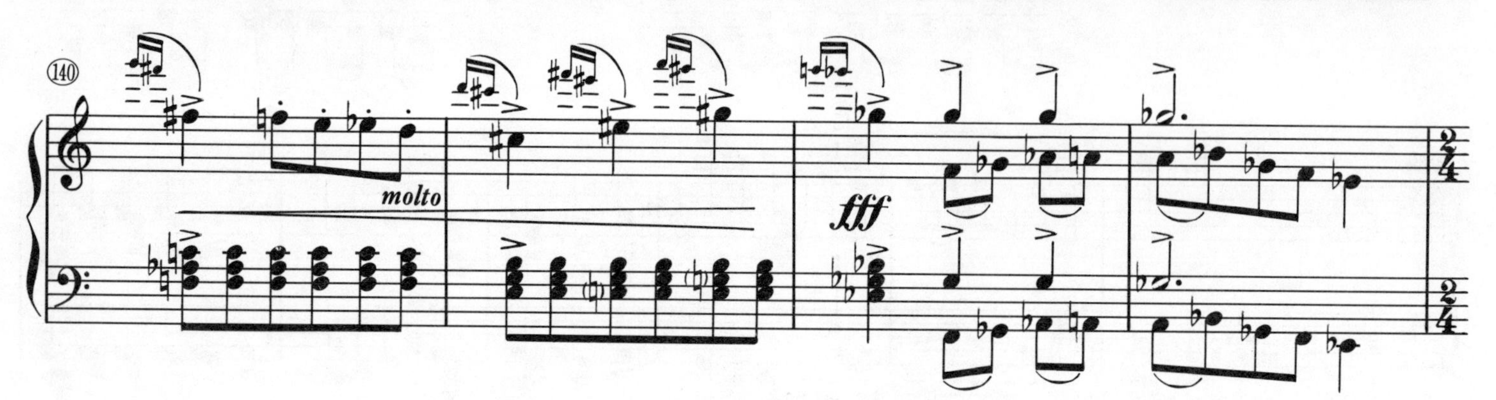
140
molto
fff

144
sfp sub.

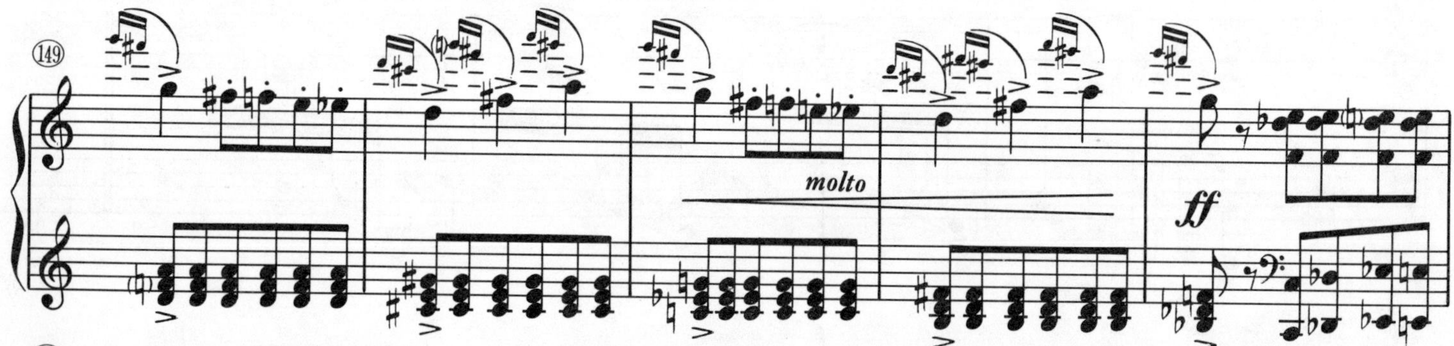
149
molto
ff

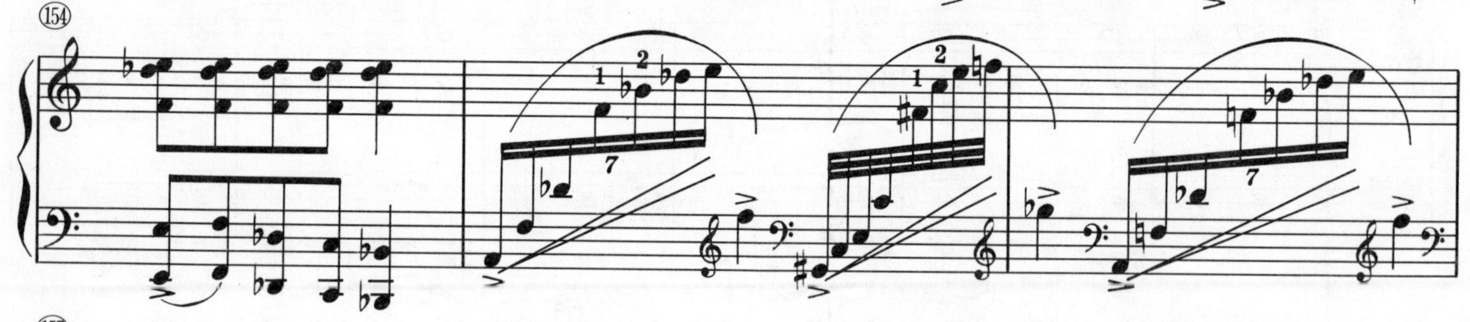
154

157

160
ff
165
169
173
177
meno f - - e cresc.
181
molto
fff
strepitoso

186

189

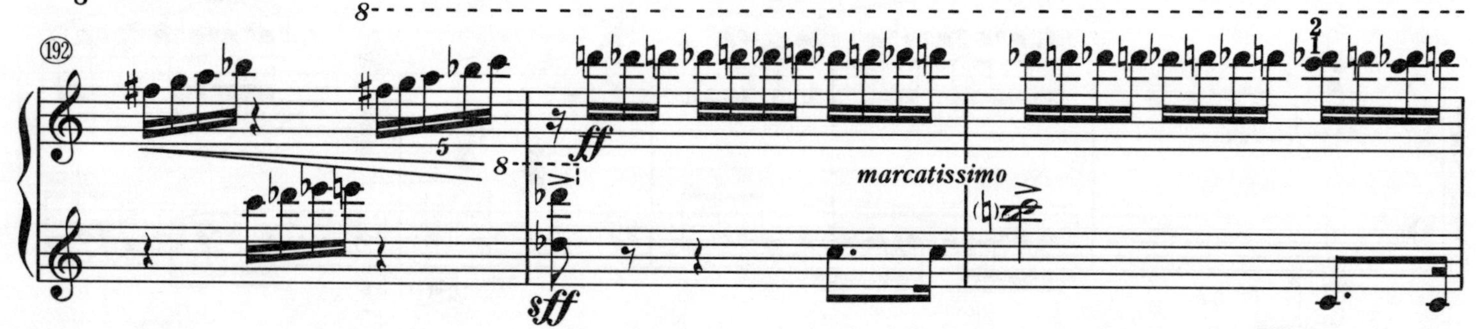
192
ff
sff
marcatissimo

195

Tempo I
197
allargando
poco ritard.
fff

201
a tempo
f
mf

206
p
poco
a

211
poco
dim.

216
pp
pp

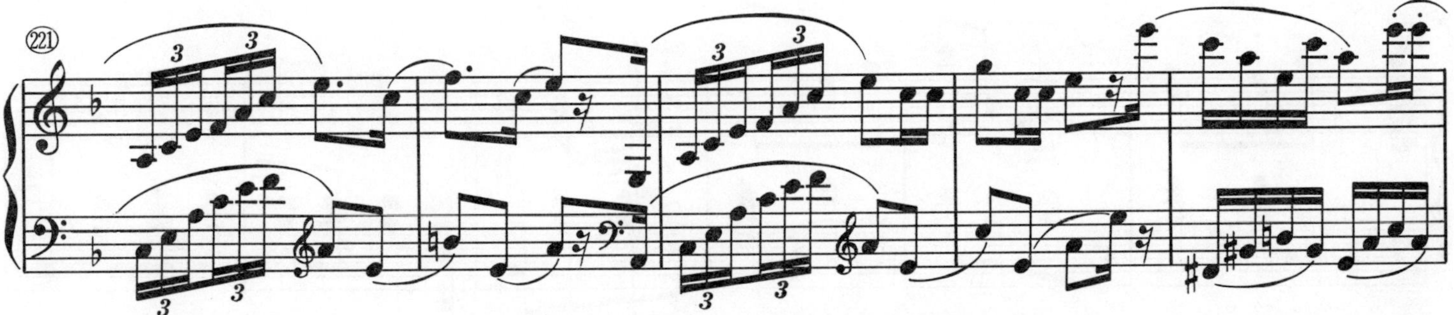
221

226
sempre
poco

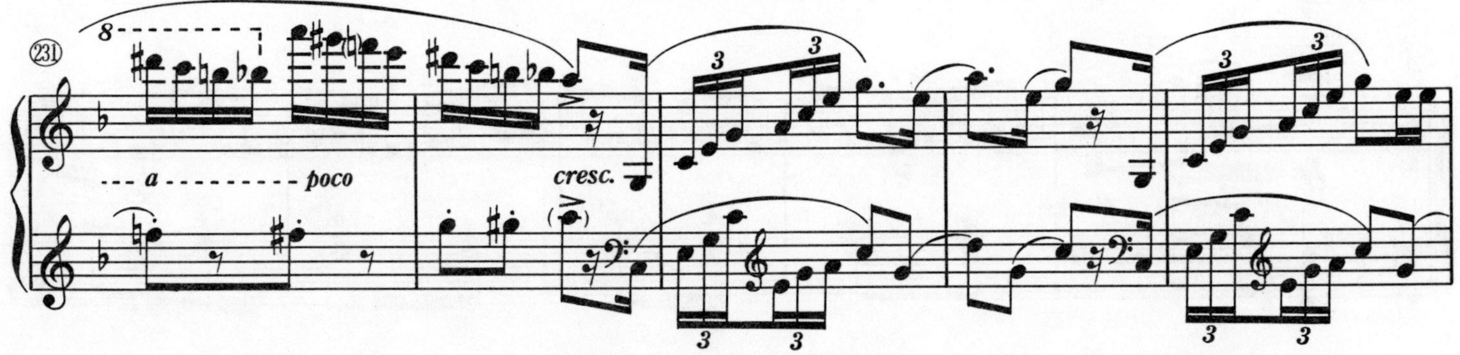
231
a
poco
cresc.

236
8

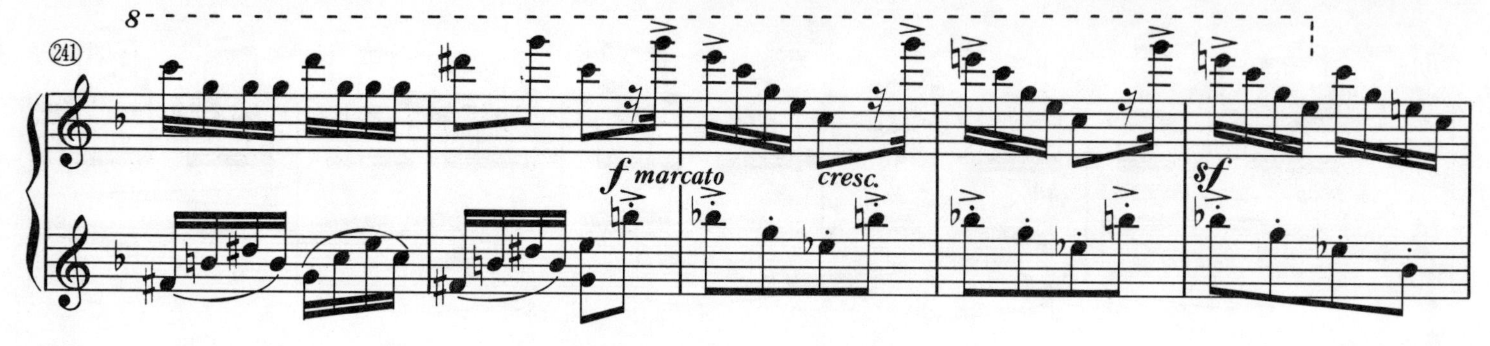
241
8
f marcato
cresc.
sf

246
sf
3
f
con brio
252

263
8
ff
p sub.

268
mf marcato

273
f

278
p sub.
cresc.

283
f

288
8

295
ff
al fine

SONATINA TOCCATA

Denes Agay

sempre legato
cantabile

cresc.

45
mp
mf

49
f
legato

53

57
p
cresc. sempre

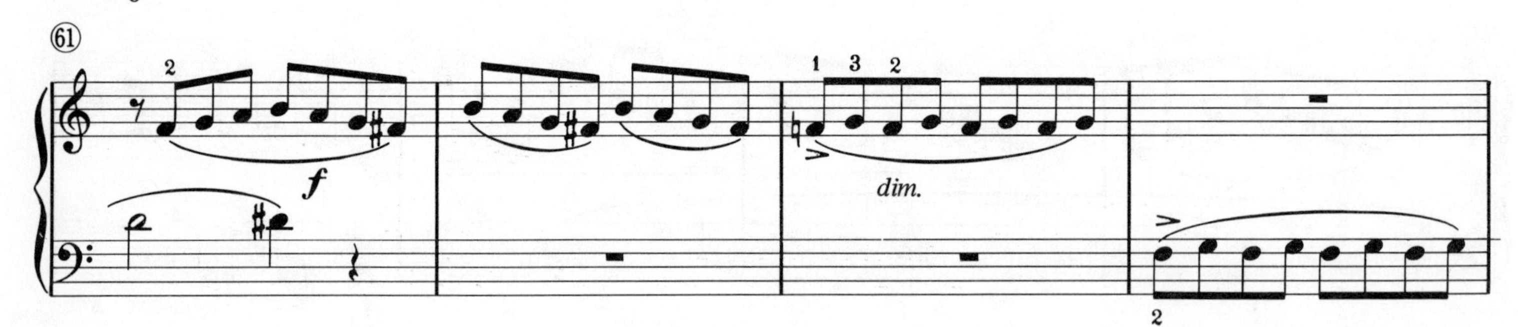
61
f
dim.

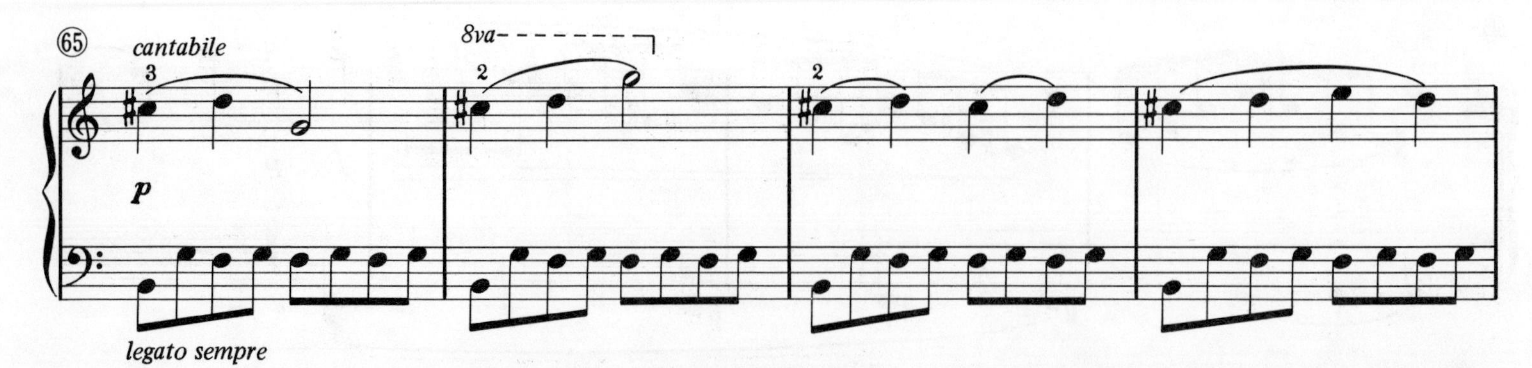
65
cantabile
8va
p
legato sempre

69
8va

73
8va

77
mf

81
f

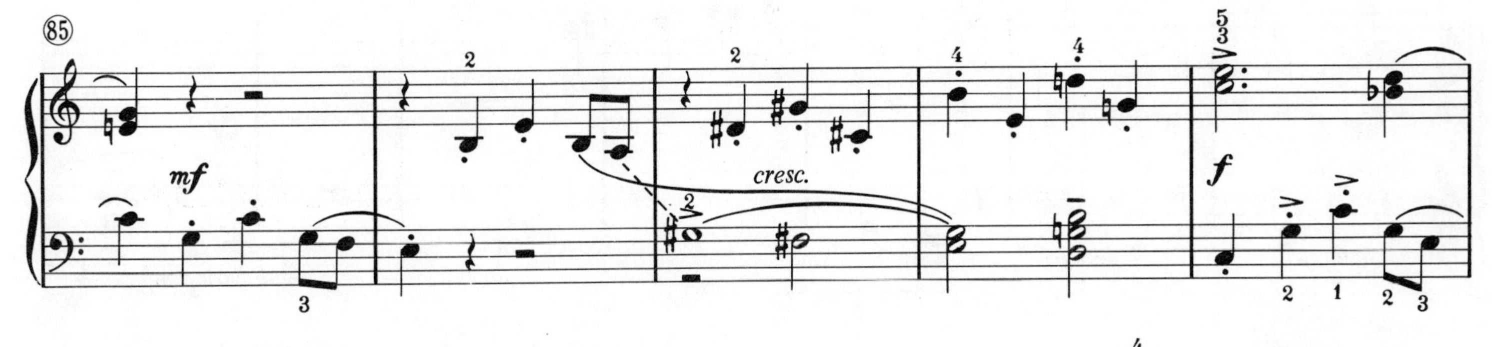
85
mf
cresc.
f

90
dim.
p
ff

SONATINA FOR YOUNG PEOPLE

(Op. 5, No. 3)

Konstantin Sorokin

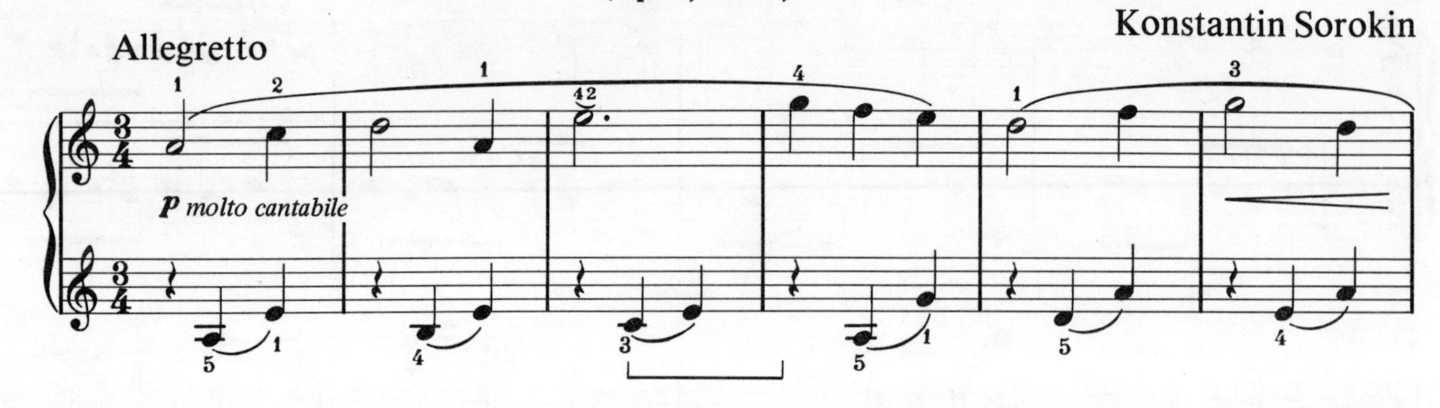

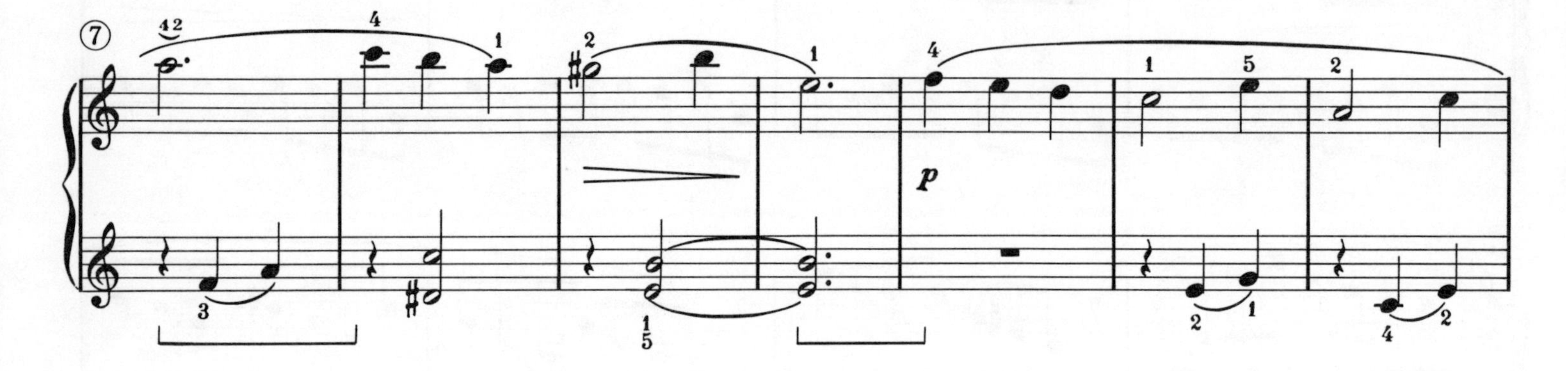

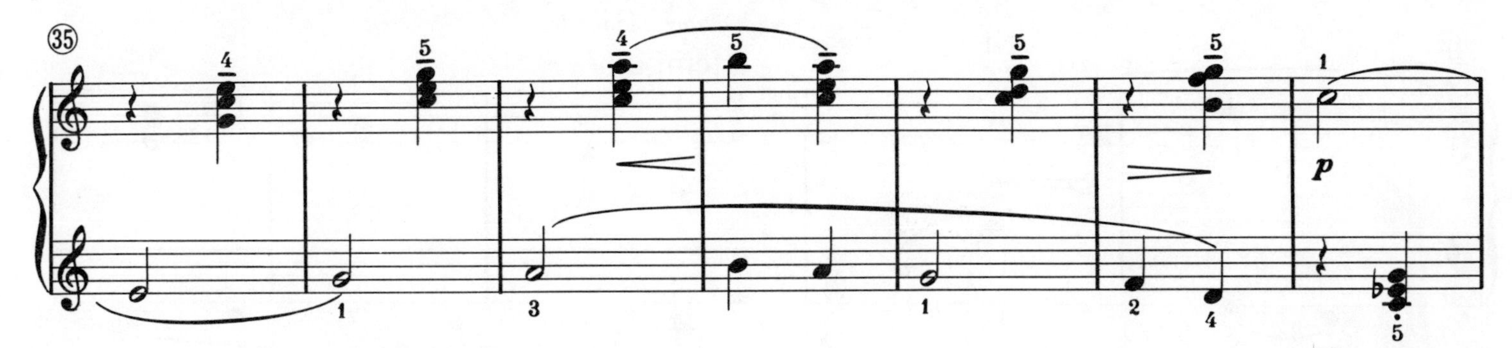

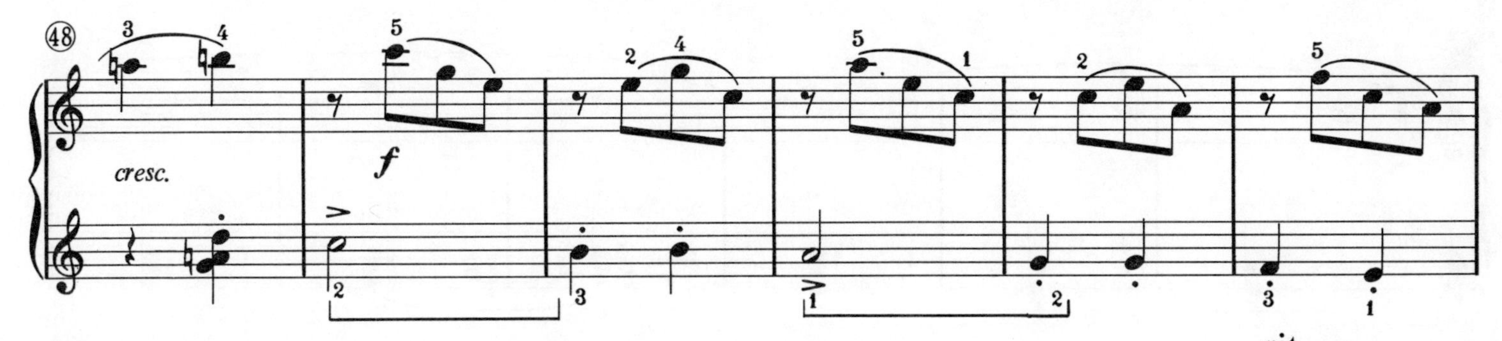
cresc.

rit.

Tempo I

71
rit.
with daring and resolve
a tempo

76

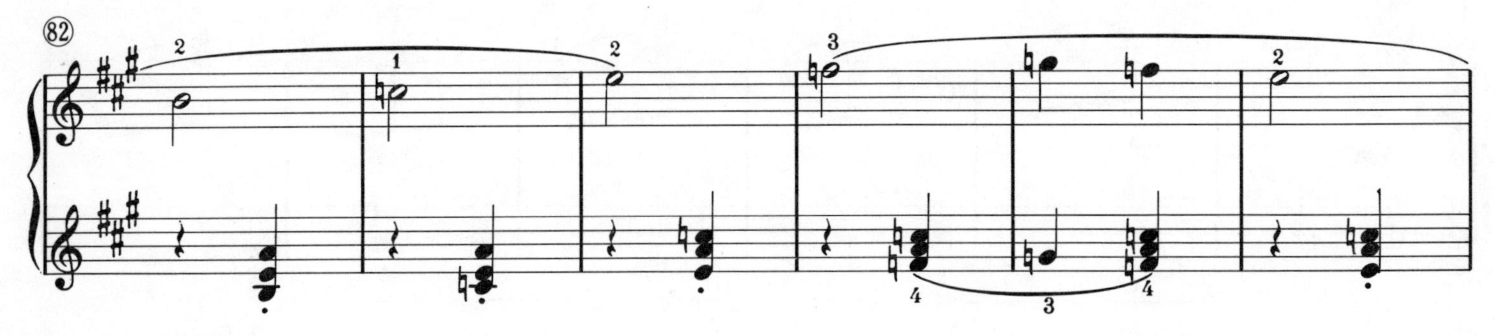
82

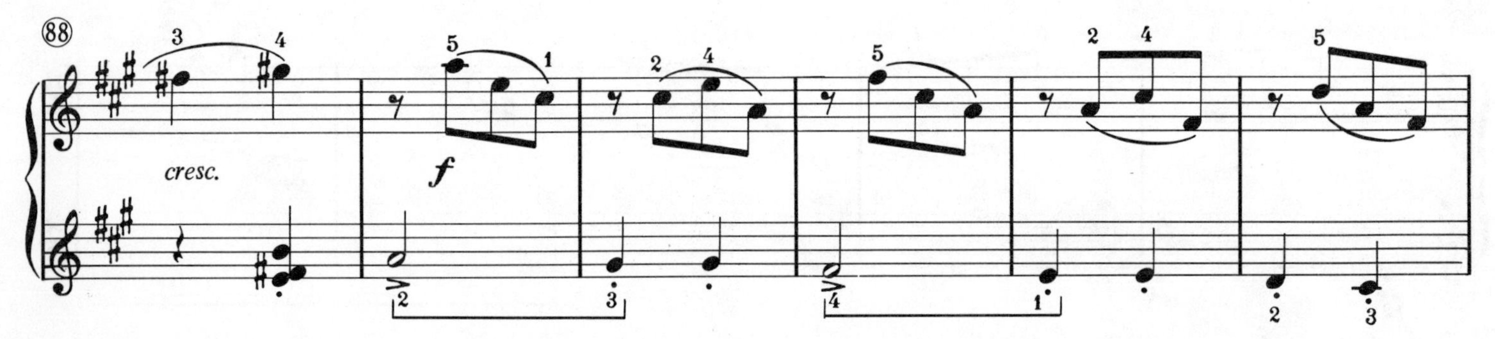
88
cresc.

94

100
cresc.
dim.